the Pits of Hell

Dear Devan and Emily,
   May the information in
this book help keep your
loved ones safe. We were
created to be Beautiful
              Amazing and
              Strong!
      Love in Jesus,
      Jenny B.A.S.
      Galatians 2:20

the Pits of Hell

Jenny B.A.S.

TATE PUBLISHING
AND ENTERPRISES, LLC

Published by Tate Publishing & Enterprises, LLC
127 E. Trade Center Terrace | Mustang, Oklahoma 73064 USA
1.888.361.9473 | www.tatepublishing.com

Tate Publishing is committed to excellence in the publishing industry. The company reflects the philosophy established by the founders, based on Psalm 68:11,
"The Lord gave the word and great was the company of those who published it."

Book design copyright © 2014 by Tate Publishing, LLC. All rights reserved.
Cover design by Joseph Emnace
Interior design by Mary Jean Archival

Published in the United States of America

ISBN: 978-1-63185-423-1
1. Biography & Autobiography / Personal Memoirs
2. Family & Relationships / Abuse / Domestic Partner Abuse
14.04.01

This book is dedicated to Robin, for all your support and encouragement and for giving me a new name. Without you, this book would not have been written. You are my hero!

To She, for not giving up on me and being there with a truck when I needed you most. I love you, Lady!

And of course, to Jesus, my loving Savior, who never left me nor forsook me.

Domestic violence is one of the most chronically underreported crimes.[1]

Ever since I was a small child, Satan has been trying to destroy me.

Flashbacks

Sabotaged by the enemy when you least expect it. Something, anything, captures your attention—an angry voice, a movement in your peripheral vision, a shadow behind you in the mirror, a lock on the door, a song, a smell, an unexpected touch. And *bam!* It hits—flashback! You are there again. Trapped! You no longer see reality. You see a foot flying at you. You hear the sneering accusations. It's sucking you into the blackness again. Can people tell what's happening? Does it show on my face? Don't flinch, blink it away, breathe. God help me! This isn't really happening! And then, it's over. I'm okay, back to reality. Someone asked me something. I didn't hear what they said. They have to repeat. Does anyone know, or do they just think I'm a space case? When will this stop? Sometimes, weeks, months pass by without one. Sometimes, it's multiple ones a day. I never know until it has me in its grip. It wears me down. But "I can do all things through Christ which strengtheneth me" (Philippians 4:13, KJV).

Prologue

Sometimes, I wonder what my life would be like if I had never met John. What if I had refused to date him. I lost so much when I died. It's hard to remember what I liked, who I was, before he came in and took over.

I have to skip over this huge, ugly, black void to see "me" before John. What things did I like? How did I dress? What did I listen to? Would I still have become an alcoholic? Possibly. Would I have gone to college and met a nice Christian guy? Or would I have fallen for the next abusive jerk to notice me? If I had known the warning signs of an abuser, would I have dumped him before it was too late? If I had known what to look for and seen it on my own, would I have left him? Not dated him at all? Every one told me he was no good, but I didn't listen.

Would Mark still be alive if I hadn't dated John? How different his life could have been! Or would it still have ended the same way? I don't know.

How do I find myself again? Looking back has limits. Alcohol haze, fear, so much time has passed. It distorts things. I don't want to be that immature, insecure teenager again. How do I fit who I really was into the woman I am now and let go of the bad?

I know I love the color orange. I recently rediscovered Dan Fogelberg. I'm over Cher and KC. I remember being physically fit. I swam, ran, and exercised. I liked to dance and loved love songs and ballads. I wrote stories. I even did art. I took modeling classes and liked to teach. I had plans, dreams, hopes. I liked camping, seeing snow, the changing of the seasons, and small towns. I hated loud music, traffic, dusting, and being out of control. I was deathly afraid of heights. I liked school and my housework. I didn't mind working hard. I liked driving much better than being a passenger. My friends and I went to the mall, we shopped and hung out. I was aware that guys thought I was hot. But I wanted to be smart. I didn't want to be used. How did I end up so stupid that I was used to the point of death? I wanted to be loved, not killed.

I want to tell my story, but only if telling it helps others. Can I do it right? So people see what an abuser looks like? So they can spot one and save themselves from hell? I don't want to tell it just to get it out of my system or to just get over it. Maybe Jesus will bless it and bring good from the bad as only *he* can do. It's too late to save Mark or me, but maybe someone else will be spared, if they have the knowledge. It's selfish to keep lifesaving information to myself. So here I go.

PART 1

Dancing around the Pits

I met John in August of 1979. It was the summer before my senior year. I was seventeen and he had just turned nineteen that month. He drove a black Trans-Am just like the one in *Smokey and the Bandit*. He was tall and slender with dark hair. I thought he was cute.

He seemed to have it all at first, except a job. Little did I know that his confidence and exuberance were fueled by drugs and alcohol. He was addicted to codeine, but I wouldn't find that out for months. [10, 13]

I had just recently confessed my deepest, darkest secret to my friend, Ruby. I was convinced that something was seriously wrong with me. Although I knew it wasn't true, I felt like the last virgin on earth. I feared a lot of things: picking the wrong guy, being used, getting pregnant, and being dumped. But mostly, I feared that I was incapable of loving at all.

Every time I dated someone, on the tenth day, it was over for me. It was like a switch had been flipped inside me. No matter how much I liked him or how nice or cute he was, on the tenth day, I would be filled with revulsion for him. I couldn't stand him, his face, his voice, holding his hand, nothing. I would find some excuse to break up with him. Or worse, just flat out dump him without a reason. I hurt a lot of guys. I honestly didn't mean to. Sometimes, I would try to ignore my changed feelings, hoping they would change back. We'd talk on the phone or go out with a group of friends, but it never worked. I was sure that I was somehow defective.

My friends just thought I was too picky. They said I should cut the guys some slack. After all, they were guys and couldn't help being unworthy of us superior females! At first, I laughed with them in agreement. But as the switch, against my will, continued to flip, I grew more afraid.

Ruby was one of my best friends. We had met freshman year in home economics. We had both just moved to Phoenix, she from Texas and me from New Mexico. We had been through a lot together in those early years. Her family had moved to Apache Junction halfway through our sophomore year, then out to Black Canyon City. We made a plan to have her attend her senior year back at Sunnyslope, so we could be together. We were successful in getting our way and felt invincible! We had several classes together when school started. We were going to spend afternoons at my house every day until her dad picked her up on his way home. Everything seemed to be working out the way we wanted it to.

When I confessed my defect to Ruby, she assured me that when "the right one" came along, it wouldn't happen. So I would know he was "the right one" and it would be okay. She didn't laugh at me, and I knew she wouldn't blab to anyone. Ah, the infinite wisdom of a seventeen-year-old! How stupid we were!

I worked at a Dairy Queen for $2 an hour and shared a station wagon with my older sister, Anita. We had to pay the insurance and our own gas. One of the girls I worked with was Darci. We went out cruising Central Avenue one night. A black Trans-Am passed us. Darci said she knew the owner. He had worked with her mom at a nursing home. His name was John. We all pulled over and talked for a while. His friend, Tom, was with him. They said they could get beer. We said we could go to my house to drink it. My parents were out of town. So that's where we ended up.

The night ended with them being mad at us for not having sex with them. We had ridden around in his car for a while. Apparently, he thought that would change my mind, but it didn't. So when he left with my phone number, I didn't expect to hear from him and that was okay. He was cute, but not gorgeous, and kind of arrogant. 16

He called a few days later and said to meet him at North Mountain Park at 10:00 p.m. on Saturday night. I had to work until 11:00 p.m. at Dairy Queen. He said, "Fine, just be there before midnight or I'll find someone else." Anita had the car, so I had to walk. I got there with five minutes to spare. I was just in time to see John making out on the hood of his car with some bleached blonde. As

I stood there staring in shock, they got in his car and left. He drove right past me and didn't even notice me. I was *furious* at myself for being stupid and at him for being a jerk! [6, 10, 25]

I started walking home. Three guys stopped and gave me a ride. I had them drop me off a block away from my house. One of them was a little creepy and I didn't want him to know where I lived.

John called again a few days later. I hung up on him. That went on for a week. Then I decided to chew him out instead of hanging up. He apologized and asked for a chance to make it up to me. I said he could take me to the movies that weekend. At this point in my life, I was used to using guys. "Use them before they try to use you!" was our motto. Since they only wanted one thing, it seemed fair to get dinner or a movie out of them. [27]

So we went to the drive-in. He insisted on taking my car. "We'll be more comfortable in your car," he reasoned. He was nice at first. He went to the snack bar and bought us sodas. He got a little peeved when I wouldn't get into the backseat. He said, "No one watches the movie at a drive-in!" I replied, "Well, I do!" As we sat there, I began to feel weird. I could actually feel my hair growing! I told John about it and he laughed. "That's just the speed," he said. He had spiked my soda with speed. I was really pissed. Sure, I partied on the weekends—drinking and a little pot—but that was it. For him to put something in my drink was *not* okay. I made him take me home. [1, 12, 18]

I figured that was the last I'd see of him. So he had a nice car, the guy was a jerk! School started and things didn't turn out quite like Ruby and I had planned. She couldn't handle the weight-lifting class we were in. We didn't need the credit, so we dropped it. We still had Foods and US Gov't together. Plus, we had the afternoons when I didn't work.

Then John called again. I was really surprised. Ruby didn't think much of him at all. He said he was trying to improve himself. He was looking up one word a day in the dictionary and memorizing the meaning. He tried to work the word *protuberant* into every sentence and it just got silly. He apologized and asked for another chance, again. Ruby and I had talked about it. I said it had been over ten days and the switch hadn't flipped. She said it wasn't ten dates though and she didn't think he deserved anymore time. After all, a jerk is a jerk. 27

But John was very hard to ignore or say no to. He called every day, multiple times. He wanted me to come over every day, but I had homework or a shift at the DQ or Ruby to hang with. He would be sad and whiny. I felt bad. It seemed he really wanted to spend time with me. I had no experience with long-term relationships, other than watching my friends and sisters. They usually ended up going out and leaving me behind. So I went out with John again. 2, 4, 9

He took me to a bar in his neighborhood that he frequented. He tampered with my license so it looked like I was nineteen, which was the legal drinking age then. We shot pool, danced to the jukebox, and drank a lot of beer. He tried to get in my pants and I resisted. I didn't know what to think of this guy. He had no job, still lived at home, played the music too loud, drank every day, but he could be sweet and funny when he wanted to be. He could be very charming and endearing. He talked a good deal about what he wanted to do. He wanted to start a band again and liked to work with electronics. He seemed like a lost little boy sometimes. I wanted to help him. He would find an empty parking lot and do doughnuts in his car, spinning tight circles as fast as he could. I hated it. It scared me to death! He would also drive backward like a maniac. He said it was fun, that I needed to learn to live a little and let go. He said I was uptight and too serious. I explained that I liked to have fun as much as the next person, but being in a car driven by a crazy person was not my idea of fun. I would ask him to let me out so he could have his fun, but he always made me stay in the car. I think he was trying to impress me with his driving skills. I wasn't impressed. His antics just made me nervous. [5, 13, 23]

Soon, I was seeing him several times a week. I didn't want to go to the bar every time. He would buy beer and we would sit at the park and talk. I told him all my hopes, dreams, plans for the future, and my fears. I thought we were getting to know each other. He was scheming. He had an older brother who had died. Sometimes, he took me to the cemetery to see his grave. He would sit there and cry. I felt sorry for him. [3, 17, 26]

John earned money by helping his older brother, Jeff, trim palm trees in the afternoon. They would go out driving around, looking for trees that needed trimming, and make thirty or forty dollars each. He would fill his tank, buy cigarettes, and spend the rest that night on booze. Sometimes, he got me a flower or a candy bar.

I thought things were going well, but John was frustrated. He said he had never gone with a girl this long and not had sex. I tried explaining my reasoning to him. I wanted to wait for the right guy, the right time and place. He said he thought I should know by now. One night at the park, we were wrestling playfully around by his car. He grabbed me in the crotch, and as a reflex, I kneed him in the nuts—hard. He grabbed a nearly full can of beer off his hood and slammed it onto the asphalt. It was smashed flat! John was really mad. When he could talk, he cussed me out. I started crying. I said I was sorry over and over. My brother, Mark, had taught me a lot of self-defense and I had acted automatically. That was the first time I saw him lose his temper. 2, 8, 13, 14, 16, 17

By this time, I had met John's family. His dad, Jeff Sr., worked as a salesman at a furniture store. His mom, Nora, was a cashier at a grocery store. His brother, Jeff, lived at home, off and on. He also had an older sister, Carla. She was divorced and had two beautiful little girls. Her boyfriend lived with her. John had not met my family. He said, "I don't *do* parents! They don't like me and I don't like them." I wasn't supposed to date anyone without my parents meeting them first. I had been telling my mom I was helping a friend with homework. I was also working on John, trying to get him to pick me up and meet my family. After all, I had met his. It seemed reasonable to me. I assured him they would like him. He did dress nice and could be polite when he wanted to be. I didn't think it was a really big deal. 1, 3, 10, 16

He met my parents one night when he came to pick me up for a "special night." We were meeting a doctor friend of his, and he wanted me to look my best. That meant a long session with the curling iron. The "Farrah Fawcett" look was still in and John liked my hair done that way. Mom was mad that day because my sisters hadn't done their chores. I ended up doing them so she would stop yelling. So I got a late start and wasn't ready when John knocked. I was supposed to be right by the door waiting for him, so I could just slip out. I didn't hear him knock, but Dad did. He answered and let John in. I was informed that he was there and about died. I knew he would be pissed. Boy, was he! He was convinced that I had set it up that way and nothing I said made any difference. He cussed me out all the way to his friend's house. I explained that Mom and Dad had liked him, and now it was all over. I was hurt that he didn't believe me about not planning the whole thing. As soon as we got to the doctor's house, he turned into a different person. He became this sweet, funny charmer who was the life of the party. It was astonishing. I had never seen anyone change moods so fast! 8, 13, 14, 16, 18, 26

The dinner with the doctor was important to John. He wanted to hook the guy up with an HBO unit in exchange for prescription drugs. John claimed to have hurt his back when he worked at the nursing home. He said he was in constant pain and the only thing that helped was codeine. He had also worked for HBO as an installer for a few months. He said they had given him some old units to play around with. He fixed them up and installed them for people. Carla's boyfriend made the convertor boxes they needed to pick up the signal. John made two hundred bucks a unit so people could get illegal HBO. Of course, he told me it wasn't illegal since HBO had given him the units. They had to know that he was going to fix and use them, so it was okay. He was such a contradiction! It was hard for me to figure him out. He kept me off balance with his mood swings. Funny and crazy one minute, serious the next, and then there was his temper. He could schmooze people really well. He almost always got what he wanted. He could talk anyone into anything it seemed. He smoothed over all my objections. No one is perfect, especially not me. Maybe I was too picky, like my friends said. So I overlooked his faults and my misgivings. I decided he had to be the *one*! It had been way more than ten days. It was already the middle of October. 13

So one night after the bar closed, we parked to make out before going home. I gave in and let him have my virginity. He was surprised that I was really saying yes. It was awful! But I chalked it up to being the first time and figured it would get better. After all, he told me that he had never had any complaints, so it must be me. 1, 8, 10

It continued to be awful. I guess part of it was my fault for the way I handled it. I was embarrassed and humiliated about the whole thing. I hadn't heard of anyone not liking sex. My friends all thought it was so great. The ladies in books saw stars. So what was wrong with me? Here I was, turning out to be defective in a different way. So I began faking it. I knew enough about how it was supposed to be to fool John into thinking he was great. Maybe it would just take a while to get used to it. I was committed to making it work. As far as I was concerned, that first time, I had married John in my heart, and he knew it. 26

He started expecting me to come over every day as soon as I got out of school. He didn't care that it left Ruby alone at my house. He resented when I worked at DQ or babysat, even though I spent my money on him. He didn't care that I had homework. John said if I would quit school like he had done, we would have more time together. He felt *he* should be my priority—not homework, jobs, friends, or anything else. He was always very persuasive. Surely, I wanted to spend more time with him, if I really loved him, that is. [1, 2, 4, 9, 10, 18]

That became his big thing, his main point. Any time I couldn't do what he wanted right then, was "proof" of me not loving him. According to John, if I loved him, I wouldn't work any shifts at DQ with another guy. But I had no control of the schedule! He said if I loved him, I would want to spend every minute with him and that I would obey him instead of making up excuses not to see him. He wanted to be my whole life, and that just wasn't possible. It was a really big bone of contention to John. [3, 4, 7, 10, 18]

I hadn't told anyone yet that we were having sex. I wanted to be able to honestly say it was great. Ruby and I had planned on my spending the night of her birthday at her house. It was a school night, but her dad would bring us to my house in the morning, just like he brought Ruby every day. So our parents were okay with it, but John was not. His car had been stolen that morning and he was devastated. (I found out later it had been repossessed for nonpayment.) I felt badly about it, but I wanted to talk privately with Ruby. I bought him an album. I think it was Styx or Journey. John really liked both those bands.

He was touched about the gift and relented about me going, as long as he had the phone number. Ruby's house didn't have a phone, so I gave him the number for her aunt who lived across the street. He called half a dozen times that night, including after 11:00 p.m., waking up her aunt. 7, 9, 26

I confessed to Ruby how horrible sex was with John. She listened sympathetically and gave me some pointers about things I could do to make it better. She, of all people, knew how I felt and how badly I needed to make this work. I felt like there was some hope. She and her boyfriend had been together quite a while and were really happy.

I told her that I felt badly about leaving her alone at my house a lot. She said she understood. My relationship with John was new. Of course, we wanted to spend time with each other. There would be other times to hang out when the newness wore off. She still didn't think much of him, but she wanted to be happy for me.

So I was at John's house every day. He would start calling as soon as he got up—about noon. I didn't get out of school until 1:30 p.m. He knew it, but called anyway, every ten to fifteen minutes. It really ticked my mom off! I would hear about it the second I got home. "Doesn't he know what time you get out of school? Tell him to quit calling before 2:00 p.m. I can't get any sewing done. Doesn't he work?" Mom would harp on me. Who would want to stay and listen to that ranting? 3, 4, 9, 26

If I said I couldn't come over until my homework was done, he wanted me to stay on the phone with him. The phone was in the kitchen/dining room. Everyone could hear our conversation and my dad only allowed us five minutes per phone call. So John would continuously call back. I wasn't getting any homework finished that way. If I said I had to work, either at DQ or babysitting, he would act hurt. He demanded to know who I was working with and got mad if it was a guy. He accused me of cheating on him. I wasn't interested in the guys at work, but that didn't seem to matter to John. I explained that I was just friends with the guys at work. John said, "Guys and girls can't be just friends." He made such a big deal about it bothering him. It didn't bother him to spend the money I made though. If I was babysitting, I had to give him the phone number where I would be. At first, it was flattering. I thought he couldn't live without me. But it got old, really fast. 3, 4, 7, 8, 9, 10, 11, 17, 18, 22

The first time we were together after Ruby's birthday, I tried one of the things she had told me about. John exploded in a rage. He was convinced I had cheated on him at Ruby's. "That's why you took so long to come to the phone. Where did you learn this? Who taught you?" he demanded. I tearfully explained that Ruby had told me. "Why would she be telling you what to do in bed with me?" he raged. "Were you talking about me with her?" Of course, I said, "Yes, girls always talk about boyfriends. She was just trying to help." He forbid me to talk about him to anyone, ever. He said he would not be gossiped about or laughed at. I promised not to, and he started to calm down. 8, 10, 11, 12, 14, 16, 18

A few days later during sex, he brought up Ruby again and asked why I had been talking to her in the first place. "What was she trying to help you with?" he asked. I nervously confessed that I still felt uncomfortable during sex and she had told me some things he might like, so it would be better for both of us. Another explosion! "So now I'm not good enough in bed for you? Who are you comparing me to, whore? You seem pretty satisfied to me. Pretty selfish, always getting off and then begging me to stop!" he raged. On and on, he went. How could I confess that I had been faking? He was so mad already. I didn't want to make him any madder. "But that's why!" I said. "It was for you, to make things better for you, since it takes you so long to be done." God, I was in over my head! I had no idea how to talk to him about sex, and I was scared to death because he was so furious. [1, 8, 12, 14, 17, 26]

Now he was mad that I thought he took too long. "Do you have someone else to see, somewhere else to go? You're with *me!* That should be all that's on your mind! Unless you're cheating on me!" he said. Then he dropped a bomb. He said he was going out with his ex-girlfriend, Chloe. I had heard a lot about her. Chloe was a model, Chloe had blonder hair than I did, Chloe was his first true love, Chloe was out of state working on a big modeling contract, etc. I was stunned! How could he go out with her when we were together? He told me, "We're together, but not 'together' together." Whatever the hell that meant! Now I was mad and very hurt, but mostly scared. What if he dumped me? [1, 6, 8, 11, 16]

The night he had his date with Chloe, I got a call from a guy I had dated a couple times the year before. I decided to go out with him. We saw a movie, and afterward, he parked. But when he tried to kiss me, I started crying. I asked him to just take me home. I couldn't cheat on John. I didn't want to be a slut.

After that, I tried even harder to please John. I tried to no avail to keep him from losing his temper. It seemed he would pick a fight every other day over nothing. He would break up with me and drive me home. But he always stopped for something on the way: gas, cigarettes, soda. When he got back in the car, he would sigh and say maybe he would give me just one more chance since he really did love me so much! It was all very calculated on his part. By the third time it happened, I knew the pattern. But I went along and didn't deviate from my part because I was afraid he really would break up with me. He knew all my fears—about being used and dumped and he used it against me. It was one way he had of keeping me in line. 6, 10, 13, 17

He made me quit working at the DQ to prove I loved him. That was a big thing with him. He was always demanding that I prove I loved him. Since he believed I had cheated on him, every minute I wasn't with him had to be accounted for to his satisfaction. Besides proving I loved him, I had to prove I wasn't cheating on him. The only way to do that was to be in his sight every second! It was impossible. 3, 7, 16, 17, 18

John made me give up my modeling career because he had lost Chloe to hers. At least that's what he said. I had worked at the DQ to earn the money for modeling school. I planned on using the modeling money to pay for college. I was going to be a tutor. It paid well, was something I enjoyed, and could be done just about anywhere. But when the agency called me in early November with a job,

John said I couldn't do it. He said, "All the photographers do is use the models for sex." I half believed him. When I was in classes, working on my portfolio, the photographer had propositioned me. He gave me his card and said to call him when I turned eighteen. He told me he could get me into *Playboy*. Like I would ever pose nude for him or anyone else! I told the teacher and he was fired. John knew all this because I had told him. So he had a point, in a way. But I assured him I wasn't interested in any dirty old man with a camera. I loved John! Besides, the job was as a dresser. We helped the models change outfits, matched all the accessories, kept shoes in pairs, etc. It paid ten dollars an hour! That was way better than DQ! The agency was working on getting me into print work with sewing pattern catalogs. You didn't have to be tall for a lot of that work. At 5'2," I knew I would never make it in runway modeling. 1, 7, 8, 10, 11, 21, 22, 25

But no! John's heart had been broken by a model once. He wasn't going to have it happen again. It was him or modeling! If I'd known that a month earlier, maybe I would have chosen modeling. But in my heart, I was committed to him for life. I broke it off with the agency. Even that didn't convince John of my love for him. He just found another thing to nag me about. What now? I had already given up birth control for him. 6, 10, 16, 17, 18

About ten days after we first had sex, Ruby and I went to Planned Parenthood to get the pill. John had a fit when I told him! "Don't you want to have my baby? How can you say you love me if you don't want my baby?" he cried. So the pills were thrown away. I did want his baby, I assured him, just not before I finished school. That was something else he felt came between us. He wanted me to quit school. I did not want to and I knew my parents wouldn't let me either. I encouraged him to get his GED. "We could study together!" I said. "It would be fun." He thought that was the stupidest thing he had ever heard. He didn't need school, he hated school, he would succeed without school! He was a big talker who drank a lot and dreamed big dreams. I just didn't see how he was going to make those dreams come true. 10, 16, 26

Then John got arrested for assault. He called me, crying like a baby, begging me to bail him out. His bail was six hundred dollars. I only had four hundred left in the bank. His mom put up the rest without his dad's knowledge. His dad had said to leave him in jail. I thought about that for half a minute. I could have some time to do my schoolwork, get some sleep, maybe even see my friends that I had been ignoring. None of my friends liked John or his influence on me. My family didn't like him either. But in the end, I bailed him out. My sister, Anita, and her boyfriend drove me to the jail. The officers said I couldn't wait for John. It would take time to process and release him. So I paid and went home. John was really mad at me. He said they released him at three in the morning and he had had to walk home in the cold. 13, 14, 16, 25

The arrest seemed to shake John up a bit. He found a business school that held data entry classes. He said he could get a job working on a computer. No heavy lifting. He started pestering his mom for the money to go. His mom paid the fifty-dollar deposit for him. His dad said, "Thank God, finally you will do something with your life!" There was one little problem though. The classes started at 9:00 in the morning. John was used to sleeping past noon every day. He made it to two classes the first week and quit. He said it was just too hard to get up that early. I tried to encourage him by saying I got up earlier than that for school. If I could do it, he could too. Maybe we shouldn't stay up so late during the week, I suggested. He agreed to give it another try, but ended up having me call in sick for him each day. He made up stories about elaborate illnesses, but I just said he was sick. I had to go to the pay phone between classes to call for him. I wasn't going to get into long conversations on top of it. When I pressed him about continuing, he got mad and said I didn't know how he felt. It was harder for him than for normal people like me. So I dropped it before he lost his temper. [16, 17, 25, 27]

I started going with him to trim palm trees. Jeff had a real job by now and let John borrow his chain saw. We scoured the neighborhoods looking for scraggly palm trees. I grew to *hate* palm trees! I have scars on my hands from being stuck by the sharp points. They almost always have something nasty living in them: ants, wasps, snakes, pigeons. The wasps were the worst. I'm allergic to them. I got stung once and John was embarrassed because it made me so sick. The lady whose trees we were trimming was concerned and made John finish by himself, so I could rest. He was mad the rest of the day because I faked being sick to get out of work. He thought I had made him look bad and accused me of milking it! This from a guy who deliberately cut his own hand with a chain saw just to get a prescription for pain meds! He also got a small settlement from the chain saw manufacturer. He claimed that the saw had kicked back on him without warning, causing him to be hurt. They paid him two hundred dollars. It was gone in a few days.[1, 4, 8, 12, 13, 14, 16, 17]

Lest you think it was all bad and ugly, there were some fun times. John taught me to play pool and I got pretty good. He would have me dress all slinky and get a guy to play against me for money. The guys always thought they could beat me, but they rarely did. He only did this with guys who were new to our hangout or if we were someplace new. Mostly, we went to one of two neighborhood bars he liked. John liked to show off and part of that was showing me off. As long as he was happy, I was happy. [18]

After spending the afternoon cutting palm trees, we would eat dinner at his house. I helped his mom clean up. She didn't have a dishwasher. Then I drove home, got ready, and came back for John. We went out every night. He claimed he wanted to take me out, show me a good time, etc. But in reality, we did what he wanted nearly always. That meant either the old folks bar with the jukebox that played country hits from the '50s and '60s or the younger crowd bar where he was Mr. Hero Stud. At the old folks bar, I ended up slow dancing with the old codgers who wanted to reminisce while he played pool and told stories. They really liked John there. They all thought he was such a nice young man and we made such a sweet couple. If it had been a good tree day, he would buy a round and tell everyone about how he had been in a band. He also talked about working in the nursing home until he hurt his back and had to quit. You would think he really loved helping people, listening to those stories.

He said he was writing a love song for me. That really got them misty eyed and sentimental. He was their very own celebrity as long as he didn't start trouble. 3, 4, 13, 17, 24

At the younger crowd bar, the stories were mostly about how good a shot he was with a .44 magnum, stunts he and his friends had lived through and, of course, the places his band had played. I don't know if people believed all his stories, but they sure liked to hear him tell them. I was quieter. I had been terribly shy when I was younger. Alcohol got me out of my shell some, but I preferred not to be in the spotlight. 10

All this going out was not having a positive effect on my schoolwork. I wasn't turning in much homework and was falling asleep in class, which meant I had no notes to study. Not that I had time to study. My teachers were concerned and tried to talk to me. I assured them I was fine. I think they cut me a lot of slack since I had always been a good student before.

I was in a pilot program that year called peer tutoring. In my junior year, three of my teachers had recommended me for it. It consisted of an early bird class where we learned about lesson plans, teaching strategies, learning disabilities, and how best to help struggling peers. Then we were in a classroom another hour, actually working with a kid who needed help. I loved it! Except for the getting up early part. It was really hard when we stayed out until two or three in the morning. But I convinced myself I wanted to have fun my senior year. I had taken AP classes for three years. My counselor told me I was number 70 in our class of over 450. She said if I worked hard this year, I could graduate in the top ten percent. It would look good for college. But I didn't have college on my mind anymore. I had only John in my thoughts.

When my first report card came, my parents weren't happy with my Bs. I hadn't been out every night with John yet and had been able to get some work done. But the second report card was worse. I was grounded for Christmas break. I managed to do a lot of catch-up work, which my teachers graciously gave me credit for. John was really upset at not being able to see me. He had me sneak out a few times. I showed Mom all the schoolwork I had done and she let me go to John's house on Christmas Eve. Our family always opened one gift on Christmas Eve and the rest in the morning. I didn't make it home Christmas morning. I was terribly hung over. John's parents were drinking Kahlua and let us have some. I had never had it before. I spent a lot of Christmas Eve in the bathroom throwing up. His mom had me spend the night. I'm not sure if she was really worried about me or worried that my parents would be mad at her for letting me drink so much. I don't remember what John and I got each other for Christmas. I do know that his mom paid for his gift to me. I bought John's with the last of my babysitting money. 4, 25

When school started up again, I resisted going back to the old routine of drinking every night. I suspected that John was an alcoholic and maybe even addicted to his prescription medication. John had seemed so clumsy or just unlucky to keep getting hurt. But after a little time away from him, I began to pay more attention. I was very concerned that he took so many pills a day and mixed them with alcohol. I had read the warnings on the label and told him it said not to drink or drive while taking them. He just laughed at me. "My doctors know what I'm doing and they said it's okay. You worry about everything. Lighten up," he said. So I kept quiet about it, but I watched. 1, 24

I told him I didn't want my grades to slip again. I asked if we could do something besides go to the bar. He relented and took me to the movies a few times. But it turned out to be the drive-in and he always brought beer and pills. We didn't watch the movie either. I said I wanted to do things with other people, include our friends, maybe even double-date with my friends. I never saw them anymore. That caused another explosion. He accused me of being bored with him, of looking for his replacement, of cheating again. We would be driving down the street, and all of a sudden, he would slam on the brakes. He would scream at me, "Should I go back? Do you want to sleep with him? Is he your newest conquest?" I had no idea what he was talking about. He said there had been someone walking and he had caught me checking them out. I never even saw the person! I told him he was crazy. He should know I loved him. I had proven it often enough, putting up with all his problems. That did it! He felt he put up with me and all my whining and complaining, all my stupid ideas, like making New Year's resolutions, blah, blah, blah. I had talked to him about making resolutions and steps he could take to make his dreams a reality. I asked how he was going to be in a band without even having an instrument. All he had was air guitar and he drummed on everything. He had taken offense, thinking I said he had no talent. He said he could be lead singer. If I didn't believe in him, I could hit the road. I reminded him I did believe in him. I was just curious how he planned on getting anywhere when basically he was doing nothing to further himself. 3, 5, 7, 8, 14, 16, 17, 26

That had turned into an argument about how I was just like his parents. They always nagged him about getting a job, paying rent, or moving out. Didn't I see him out there every day working his ass off trimming trees? Why couldn't I get off his back? Show him some consideration? After all, he was practically a cripple from pain most of the time. He said nobody cared about him. His parents would just let him die like they did his brother, James. Apparently, James had complained for weeks of severe headaches. He had insisted their parents pay for extensive medical tests, which they refused to do. He was in his twenties, living on his own, and could pay for his own tests. He died of a brain aneurism a few weeks later. John never forgave his parents for that. He had worshiped James. 15, 17, 27

Now it seemed he was determined to make history repeat itself. Sometimes, he would veer into the oncoming lane, yelling that he wanted to die. I would grab the wheel and try to keep us from crashing. If I was driving and we got into a disagreement, he would stomp his foot over mine on the accelerator and jerk the wheel into oncoming traffic. "If you don't love me, I don't want to live!" he would yell. "And if I go, you go because I can't stand the thought of someone else having you!" I was already nervous being in cars, having grown up with my dad. I considered Dad to be a pretty crazy driver. John's antics did not ease my mind. He ended up winning all arguments because I was too afraid to make him mad. 5, 14, 15, 16, 17, 20, 25, 26

Something I haven't mentioned yet is how much my brother, Mark, hated John. We had been really close before I started dating him. Mark knew that John was my first real boyfriend and he hated him for that. Also being seven years older than me, I'm sure he could tell John was no good. Mark hated seeing me waste my life on John. Of all my family, Mark hated John the most.

John's mom was trying to help with that problem. She had my family over for dinner and tried to get to know them. That seemed to just give John more things to pick on my family about. Oh, he was polite to their faces, but he mocked them horribly behind their backs. That was something he did even to his own friends, so I didn't think too much about it. I didn't like it though. If I told him so, he would be offended. He said that proved I was on their side and not his. He especially made fun of my mom and said I should try not to be like her. He was so dramatic and extreme. There was only one way to view things—*his* way! 10

He had found a car for cheap and let me drive it home every night. This eased my mind about him driving under the influence. It also freed him up to not drive me home and chance running into angry parents. He always insisted I call to let him know I got home safe, no matter that it was three o'clock in the morning. Besides the phone in the kitchen, there was one in my parent's bedroom. It always made a noise when the kitchen phone was picked up. That would wake up my mom and I got in trouble. I told John this, but he still insisted that I call every night.

Plus, he demanded I get over to his house as soon as I got home from school since I had his car. He needed it so we could go cut trees, after all. What had seemed like a good solution to his problem quickly turned into a trap.

4, 9, 11, 16, 18

In February, I was at John's house doing homework. We drank a couple beers. Actually, John had a lot, I had a couple. I fell asleep on the way home and crashed into a big light pole on the frontage road of the freeway. I had only minor injuries, but John's car was totaled. The cops had dropped me off at home around four in the morning. I wrote my mom a note to not wake me for school. Boy, was she shocked when she found me all bloody and passed out on my bed!

John wanted to know what his car looked like and I couldn't tell him. The cops didn't let me look at it. All I remembered was hearing them say to each other, "Did you see those teeth marks on the dash?" My mouth hurt and my lips were swollen, but I didn't have buck teeth anymore! So John had the car towed to his house. We were in the driveway with Jeff and his girlfriend when the tow truck pulled up. Totaled was right! I had wrapped that station wagon around the pole. I fainted when I saw it. John ran to his car, crying like a baby. Jeff caught me before I hit the concrete and took me in the house. He left me on the couch with his girl and went to chew John out. I felt awful about wrecking John's car. I know he blamed me, but everyone else said it was his fault. His mom said he shouldn't have been keeping me out late on school nights and should have been driving me home. That really made John mad, especially since she said it in front of their whole family. In John's mind, *nothing* was ever his fault. I refused to drive after that and didn't drive again until I was twenty-five. 1, 17

My parents grounded me for a month during which I was able to get caught up with my schoolwork. I'm sure I was nowhere near number 70 in our class by that time! We went back to using my parent's old station wagon that I had shared with Anita. She had moved in with her boyfriend and didn't need it anymore. My focus became how to make it up to John that I had wrecked his car. He expected more faithful obedience to his demands. No more was I allowed to suggest alternate ideas or protest what he wanted to do. 16

John's mom and sister were always encouraging me to stand up to him. "Say no if you don't want to do what he wants," they said. Even before the wreck, that had been hard; now, it was impossible. He was like a dog with a bone. He pestered, cajoled, begged, and came up with an endless supply of arguments to get his way. If it was something he wanted me to do in the future, he kept at me for days until I would finally relent. That had been before the accident; now, he just reminded me how much I owed him and he won. The only fights I won was about driving. He would stop the car and try to make me move into the driver's seat, but it didn't work. I absolutely refused to drive. 8

That meant he had to come get me at my parent's house. They didn't want me to see him anymore. I would wear my bathrobe over my clothes and go out front for a smoke. John would come by and I would be gone. After the accident, all discussion of us having real dates was gone. We went to the bar he liked, did what he wanted, and that was it. If he told me to dance with an old geezer, I did. I dressed the way he wanted me to, backed up his stories, and didn't argue. [8, 16, 18]

He really pushed me to drink a lot. I didn't like beer much, but he said mixed drinks were too expensive, so I had gotten used to beer. He was always topping off my beer and ordering another pitcher. If I said I had had enough, he told me to go throw up in the bathroom and start over. "That's how the biker chicks do it!" he said. It didn't matter that I wasn't a biker chick, nor did I want to be one. He didn't even have a bike! But he rode Jeff's sometimes and thought bikers were cool. He also thought if I got drunk enough, the sex would be good. That had turned into something I just endured. I was relieved on the rare nights when it didn't happen. [1, 8, 16]

I was convinced that nothing could help in that area. He had conditioned me into such a state that it was impossible to enjoy sex with him. I thought it was mostly me. I had no idea that he didn't know what to do with a lady. Then I found out he was experimenting on me. In the beginning, if I moved or touched him in a provocative way, he accused me of cheating. He used the "who taught you that?" line. If I replied that I had read it in a book or thought of it myself, he didn't believe me. He started insinuating that I hadn't been a virgin when we met. [8, 24]

In order to prove my innocence, I had to lay still and follow his instructions to the letter. He said he was going to teach me the ways of love. In order to teach properly, he felt he needed to hold an erection for a long time. So he snuck his dad's Preparation H and used it on his penis. Then he blamed me for his failure to be properly stimulated by my attempts to follow his directions. For a long time, I didn't know about this and really thought I was inept and unsexy. I was pissed when I caught John using his dad's stuff. I suggested that his numbing himself is what kept him from having satisfaction. That was met with derision and scorn. Who was I to imply he didn't know what he was doing? If I really had been a virgin, I wouldn't know any of this stuff. Besides, he reminded me that he had never had any complaints before. Sometimes, he stopped in the middle of sex. He would look thoughtful and stare at me. Then he would ask if I had cheated on him. He said I felt "a little loose" to him. If I hadn't been with anyone else, I should be tight. What a crock! But I didn't know any better or about his Preparation H. I would be devastated that he thought I was cheating. So I was usually a nervous wreck during sex, not knowing what would set him off or how long I would have to endure his attentions. I was still faking it, so he thought I was getting off. He would just keep going for hours, it seemed. I would be raw and sore and would beg him to stop. This, of course, made John mad. He said I was being selfish. I only cared about myself and not him at all. I didn't know how to please him or what to do to change the situation. I didn't confide in anyone about it either. I felt humiliated and lost. [7, 8, 12, 16, 26]

He bought those specialty condoms from the bar bathroom. With no lubricant, they just tore me up. I hated them! He acted like he had gone to a lot of trouble to get them just for me, and here I was, unappreciative again. John said he didn't know what he was going to do with me. I was such a problem for him and he hinted that he was losing patience with my hang-ups. This was a thinly veiled threat to dump me. I did what I could to try and keep him happy. 6

At Easter, John surprised me with two baby chicks. I was thrilled! They were so cute and fluffy. But it soon became a problem. We lived in the middle of Phoenix. The chicks couldn't stay in the house. I had to get special food for them. If I mentioned any of this to John, he exploded. I didn't appreciate any of his gifts. All I did was expect him to lavish me with presents and then complain about them. Gifts and favors from John often caused the recipient a lot of trouble. He never looked at the long-term implications of what he was giving. He didn't want to hear of any negative consequences that came about because of his gifts. He expected eternal, lavish praise and gratitude. 12, 14, 15, 16, 17, 18

As weary as I was with the way things were going, I felt maybe they would get better after I graduated. I had kept quiet about John's drug use since the accident. But I was still paying attention to it. I really felt he was addicted to the prescription drugs. I convinced myself that was the problem. If I could get him to get help, things would be better. Surely, it was the drugs that caused his mood swings and violent temper. I was biding my time until graduation, hoping things would settle down so I could confront him about this. I was sure his parents would side with me and we could get him the help he needed.

We were still doing the palm tree cutting thing most days. One day in mid-May, we had a really good day. John gave me most of the money to save. He said it was for my graduation gift. He said he trusted me to keep it since I was a saver and not a spender like him. I had to promise not to give it back, no matter how much he pleaded. I had the money about a week. We were out with his friend Tom and his girlfriend, in Tom's truck. Tom wanted to go someplace that was more expensive than our usual hangout. 22

So John wanted the money. He pestered me quietly and I held my ground, at first. But I knew that he would be mad if I made him look bad in front of his friend. So I gave in and we drove to my house. John made a big deal about how I was his "banker" and kept his money for him. Tom parked in front, and I ran in to get the money. Mark was over, and he followed me out of the house. I guess my parents had been filling him in on what was going on lately. He tried to pick a fight with me. I just kept going to the truck. I didn't want a confrontation, but Mark had been drinking. He was looking for a fight. Mom had followed us out of the house and was standing just behind Mark. 10, 22, 24

He was yelling at me about not being respectful to Mom and Dad. Mom was trying to calm Mark down. John got out of the truck to let me get in, and Mark started in on him. Saying he had ruined my life and was a worthless bum. He wanted to kick John's butt. John got back in the truck and closed the door, but the window was down. I leaned past Tom's girl and told him to leave. I could hear Mark yelling and Mom saying "No, Mark, don't hit him!" I turned around and saw John leaning over. He sat up and pulled his hand away from his face. His nose was bleeding. I screamed at Tom, "Go, go, go!" He floored it and we drove to a pay phone. John called the cops and said he wanted to press charges against Mark for assault.

We all ended up back at my parent's house. The cops took statements from everyone. They said we would be notified of the court date. Mom wanted me to stay, but I left. I had turned eighteen the week before and she couldn't make me stay. I spent the night at John's, wearing a pair of his ugly green scrubs for pajamas.

After that, John alternately sweet-talked and threatened me about testifying. I hadn't seen Mark hit him, though I firmly believed he did. But I told John I wouldn't say I had seen it. I was facing Tom. No one had seen John get punched. Mark swore he had swung and Mom grabbed his arm, making him miss. My refusal to lie on the stand caused a lot of fights between me and John. He would have us "practice" my testimony. He'd seat me in a chair, swear me in, and pretend to be his lawyer. He would grill me dramatically and mercilessly. But I held my ground about lying on the stand. 16, 17

The court date kept getting pushed back. After I graduated, John started complaining that Mark was prank calling him. First, he said it was hang-up calls, then heavy breathing. Finally, he claimed Mark threatened him to drop the assault charges. So John pressed charges against Mark for that. He wanted me to lie and say I had heard the calls. I hadn't, of course, because they never happened. First, he said, if I admitted I had seen Mark hit him, he wouldn't press the threatening phone call charges. But I wouldn't lie and I didn't think the cops would do much. It was John's word against Mark's. Since I knew the calls were faked and couldn't be proved, I didn't think it was serious. But John was an amazing actor. The cops bought his story, hook, line, and sinker! So now it was my fault that Mark had more charges to face, which meant more court dates. This required more time off work and an explanation to his boss. Mark had witnesses who were with him the night he supposedly called John. They testified that he had not made any phone calls. There were no phone records showing a call to John's house from the place Mark had been. But for some reason, the judge believed John. Mark was found guilty, fined, and put on probation for something he did *not* do! I was astounded. 16, 20, 21

We had fallen into a new routine after graduation. I could sleep in later. We still went out and trimmed trees for spending money. That's all we ever had, a little cash to get through the day. It never was enough with John's drugs and booze having priority. Talking to John about being addicted went nowhere. He claimed prescription drugs weren't addicting. They weren't the same as street drugs. They were safe and he needed them. He tried to get me to take them to prove how safe they were. I refused. He crushed them up and put the powder in my beer. That was a disaster! I had a terrible reaction every time he did it. John said I got sick on purpose because I wanted him to stop taking them. That I tried to make him believe the drugs were bad by faking sick. I didn't even know he was sneaking them in my drink until I had the reaction! It was not all in my head like he said. He was making less and less sense. John left me on the ground at a desert party one night after he had drugged me. His friend put me in his truck to rest until we went home. I insisted that the drugs were bad for me and begged John to stop drugging me. He wanted me to get addicted and crave them like he did, so he could point the finger at me instead of admitting his own addiction. 1, 4, 16, 18, 21

John wanted me to move into his parent's house, so he could be with me all the time. His mom put her foot down and said no to that. He tried to convince her I could do all her housework, but she held her ground this time. I was secretly glad. Summer dragged on like this. I felt we were trapped in a rut. I should have been getting ready for college, but that seemed out of reach anymore. Anita was getting married in August. I was a bridesmaid. It was very uncomfortable being around my family. It seemed everyone was mad at me, and I couldn't blame them. As soon as the wedding was over, I had to leave. I missed the whole reception. John had not been invited and was ticked about it, not that he would have attended. He said my family would never accept him. 1, 16, 17, 18, 25

An aunt from California was here for the wedding and wanted to go to Kansas to see more family. Mom wanted me to go with them. John had a fit about it. I explained that maybe if he loosened up a bit and let me go, they might see him in a better light. I told him how bad it was at home with everyone mad at me. I loved him and wanted to be on his side, but I was stuck in the middle. He decided I could go. I had planted a vegetable garden in his parent's backyard. I encouraged him to water it while I was gone. The corn would be ready when I got back and we could have a feast. John said he couldn't guarantee that we would be together when I got back. That sounded ominous. I was gone a week. The garden was dried out and dead. John hadn't watered it once. I felt like it looked. I was really disappointed and depressed. John said it was my parent's fault for taking me away from him. He said without me, he would die like the garden had. 6, 17, 21

While I had been in Kansas, I had time to think. I observed my cousins and their relationships. Respect, humor, consideration of each other was very evident. It was a hard thing to realize there was *none* of that in my relationship with John. I felt so trapped. To break up with him would leave me alone and no longer a virgin. My college plans were ruined. I had no modeling career left. I was so stubborn. I didn't want everyone to say, "I told you so!" I would have to admit I was wrong and they were right. My pride balked at that. Surely, I could make this work. I was smart and strong. There had to be a way.

When I got back to Phoenix, John had another car. It was old, but in really good shape. His mom paid for it. I can't imagine how much he bugged her that week! John had been used to us having my car and never bothered to save for his own. He said he had missed me tons. He was even pretty nice for a while. He had the bright idea that I should go to the data entry school. He had even called them and talked them into letting me use the fifty-dollar deposit his mom had paid last spring as mine. Then I could get a good job and we could get our own place. He made lots of promises I didn't believe. He was back to dreaming big dreams. I felt kind of lost and numb, but I knew I had to do something. I started wondering if I would be better off without John. I was not happy about his plans. I hated typing and wasn't good at it. I did not want to go to this school, but maybe, I could salvage something from my life and still be successful. It was as if he could read my mind. He did what he knew would keep me in line. 1, 16, 18

He called me one day just after I came back. He was at a pay phone outside his favorite hangout. While on the phone, he pretended to be attacked by Mark and a gang of his friends. He claimed they hit him in the head with a baseball bat. At this point in our relationship, I could pretty much tell when he was acting or making things up. I knew in my heart that he was making this all up. He called the cops. They were suspicious, but filed the report. So now, there was another false set of charges. The cops went to Mark's work again to question him. He was furious and humiliated. Then John threw me a bone. If I agreed to go to the data entry school without complaint, he would drop this new set of charges. So I started at the school the next week. I didn't hold out much hope for my typing skills, but I felt I owed Mark a break. 17, 20

The business school promised they would have you ready to be employed in a month. It took me six weeks to type fast enough to get a job. I did find a job quickly at a Title Plant on the night shift. This seemed to suit John just fine. He partied while I worked, then he picked me up from work to mess with me until he got tired. I could sleep in until about 1:00 before I had to get ready for the bus to go to work again. He dropped the second set of assault charges and promptly forgot all about him getting a job or us getting our own place. He was content with the way things were.

John's mom saw that I was really trying. She started to get on him about seriously growing up and getting a job. She still encouraged me to stand up to him. It seemed she really liked me. At his family get-togethers, she would introduce me as her daughter. She tried to show me how to iron. John insisted on all his clothes being ironed—even the socks and underwear! His mom ironed everything—clothes, sheets, towels! I refused to iron for John. Most of it was wash and wear. I felt it didn't need ironing, and if he wanted it done, then he could do it! I hated ironing! I stood up to him like she told me to. John let it go for a while, but he would keep coming back to the subject every few weeks. 8

We fell into a new routine once again. He would pick me up from work to party each night. I worked Sunday-Thursday with the weekends off. If we got really behind on work, we went in on Saturday afternoon for a few hours. Otherwise, I was with John most of the weekends. What money I earned was spent by him for booze, pills, and gas. I had nothing for myself. I felt it was time to address his addictions again. His parents sided with me. They were tired of him at home. He was the youngest and a mooch. They wanted him out of the house. It was a loud, terrible fight. He stuck to his story that prescription drugs are not addicting. He said his doctors assured them of this. He claimed we were stupid and mean and didn't know anything about it. I hate confrontations, especially loud, violent ones. His dad and he frequently got into shouting matches where his dad chased him through the house, trying to kick his ass. That was just for wearing a baseball cap at the dinner table. His mom and I always sat in silence, choking down our food and waiting for it to be over. She always acted like nothing had ever happened. My parents had rarely ever fought or raised their voices to each other. I was out of my element, but desperately needed his parent's support. They said they could not get him into any treatment until he admitted to his addiction. He steadfastly refused to discuss it further. So we were at a stalemate. 18, 22, 26

Then John started planning in earnest his attack for the original assault charges. That had dragged on with one postponement after another. Each time, Mark had to take off work. If he didn't show up for court, he would be in contempt. I could tell John delighted in toying with him. This really worried me. If Mark could be convicted so easily when he was innocent, what would happen when he was really guilty? At this time, I still believed Mark had hit John. But I didn't want him to go to jail! I didn't know what to do and felt powerless. John still wanted me to lie and say I saw Mark hit him. I still refused, so he kept me out of the loop about what was going on with the court date.

As Christmas approached, John put on a show of being nice. He drove me and my sister, Corinne, to buy gifts. He even let me keep some of my money to purchase them with! He stopped making so many demands and even tried being tender during sex. I was very much on guard. I felt like I was waiting for the ax to fall and cut my world to pieces. It fell on Christmas Eve. Again, I don't remember what I got John. He had been hinting that he got me something very nice. Of course, his mom had paid for it. He still was unemployed and not the least concerned about that. He had given up on the palm tree cutting as soon as I got a full-time job. He shoplifted stuff and took it back to the store to get a refund. He would claim it had been a gift, to explain why he had no receipt. Since it was unopened, the store would accept it. But even this had limits, and he still spent most of my money.

Just before we opened presents, John told me I had to read his card first and do exactly what it said. If I didn't follow his instructions exactly, in the correct order, he would be really pissed. And he said his mom would be so disappointed. I surely didn't want to hurt his mom, did I? After all, she had loaned him the money for my gift! So I opened the envelope and read the card. John had moved across the room from me and was watching like a hawk. As I read what he had written, I began to feel trapped. His first instruction was to read all the instructions, then open the box and follow to the letter all of his directions in exact order. He was proposing to me without having to say anything out loud. There was a ring in the box. I was supposed to gasp, look up at him, tear up, put the ring on my finger, look up again, smile, and nod yes. Then he would whoop and say, "I'm getting married!" and that would be it. He actually wrote what he was going to do on the card. 16, 18, 26

So I knew there was a ring in the box. Suddenly, I questioned in my mind if I really wanted to be with John for the rest of my life. My hands started shaking. I chugged my drink. Oops! That's not in the directions! I opened the box and stared at this ring that seemed to symbolize my doom. I realized I wasn't following John's directions and looked up. He was livid! He stood there rigidly waiting to see my next move. I thought of that anger directed at Mark. I put the ring on my finger. John stomped across the room, grabbed my wrist, and sneered in my ear, "You have some explaining to do!" He pulled me outside and demanded to know what that little show was all about! I stammered that a guy can't dictate a girl's reaction when he's proposing. It's an emotional time and he caught me off guard. "It was so unexpected!" I protested. I reasoned with him that since he had hinted at dumping me so often, I had despaired of him asking me to marry him. He seemed to buy it and we went back inside. He became the charming guy who was excited about being engaged. His parents and brother were congratulatory, but his sister warned that we were so young. She cautioned us to not make the same mistakes she had made. I sat there drinking and thinking that I had never even said yes! 10, 13, 14, 16, 26

The rest of the night is a blur for me. I drank way too much. I spent the night again in those stupid green scrubs. He seemed to have an unending supply of them. I wondered how many he had stolen from the nursing home. He liked to pretend he was a doctor. The scrubs were way too big for me, stiff and itchy, and such an ugly color. I had no fondness for them.

When I got home in the morning, there was a stack of presents waiting for me to open. My family may not have been speaking to me much, but they still loved me. I was so moved, I broke down and couldn't stop crying. My parents saw the ring on my finger and were concerned. "Please don't do anything rash!" they begged me. As I cried and cried, I realized how much they had tried to support me, tried to welcome John, and been rebuffed. I thought of all I had given up for him. The allowances I had made, the compromises and excuses. I thought of Mark. He was getting married in June. I barely knew his fiancée. The distance and coldness between Mark and me broke my heart. We had been so close before John. Now we didn't speak at all to each other. 3

I was supposed to shower and change clothes, then call John when I was ready. He wanted to take me to the bar to show off the ring and make the big announcement to all his drinking buddies. He called and I could barely talk. I think my family sensed the magnitude of my quandary. They retreated to the den so I could have privacy. John wanted to know what was taking me so long. Surely, he had given me plenty of time to shower and change. (No allowance had been given to open gifts or spend time with my family on Christmas.) I poured out my heart to him, going on about how loving and patient my family had been. How Mark had suffered enough. Couldn't John just leave him alone? He had already been convicted of something we all knew he hadn't done. When would it end? I couldn't live like this anymore I said. I went on hysterically, unable to stop. John tried to reason with me, but I demanded he stop hurting Mark. "I won't marry you if you keep this up!" I said. "I want peace. I want our families to like each other. No more fighting! I can't take it! I will kill myself!" I was really on the edge of a breakdown and he seemed to realize it. 10, 16

He promised to drop the charges. I told him I wouldn't wear his ring until they were officially dropped and all this drama was over. So he talked to his lawyer, who talked to the police and prosecutor. Papers were drawn up. John and I met Mark and his fiancée, Donna, at a pizza place on January 17. We ordered beer and pizza, talked awkwardly, and signed an official agreement dropping the assault charges from last May. We didn't stay long. John was charming and tried to be funny. The rest of us were uncomfortable. I could tell Mark didn't trust John, but I was sure this was the end of it. I was wrong, as usual.

Things had been different between John and me since Christmas. It had never occurred to me that John might really be afraid of losing me. He knew all along that I feared being dumped. He had always said, "No one dumps me!" Chloe had broken up with him once, he claimed. He made a great show of telling me how he had pursued her and won her back. Then two weeks later, at a party, he dumped her in front of all his friends. His pride wouldn't let him be made a fool of by anyone! I had always tried to keep the peace in our relationship. I didn't start fights, tried smoothing things out. I felt I had to be patient with this guy who only seemed to think about himself. I remembered that he was the baby of his family. He was used to loud fights. He grew up that way and didn't know any better. I felt I needed to show him a different perspective. But all my previous attempts to help him manage his temper had failed. He had flat out rejected them, ridiculed me repeatedly. Instead, he had sucked me into his world where I walked on eggshells to avoid his violent outbursts. 7, 10

The idea of actually marrying him and living like this the rest of my life shocked some sense into me. I began to go back and look at our relationship with new eyes. I realized I did not like what I saw. As I thought over things that had happened, I started resenting John. How he had talked me into compromising my principles, how he mocked my feelings, and tried to make my family the bad guys. With the charges being dropped, I felt safe to make some requests. We started going out with Jeff and his girlfriend a few times a month. This was John's concession to my request for spending time with family. As we discussed plans for the evening, I would make a suggestion that did not involve a bar. I thought of mini-golf or a movie or just window shopping at a mall. John always shot down my ideas. Now I stood up to him. I was tired of drinking every night at the same place. John was embarrassed at my openly rebellious attitude, especially in front of his brother. Jeff even told him one night that I needed to have some sense slapped into me. He said his girlfriend would never dare to defy him! I was outraged at his comment. Up to this point, John had not hit me. He had pushed me or grabbed my wrist, trying to keep me from leaving during a disagreement or argument. But he had never struck me. Deep down, I was afraid someday he would. I was right. 23

As the winter wore on, our arguments increased. John tried giving me gifts. It had worked before to win me over, but not this time. The ferret he gave me took some of my time to care for it. He resented that. But it didn't stop him from giving me rabbits. They also required care, which took my time away from him. When he complained about it, I asked why he kept giving me pets to take care of. He had to know they needed to be fed and cleaned up after. Then he yelled that I didn't appreciate anything he gave me! He said he knew I loved pets and tried to bring me joy by providing them. How could I be so selfish and blind? He started coming in to my parent's house when he dropped me off in the middle of the night. Often, he woke up my mom and dad or sisters. 1, 18, 19, 21

He began claiming to have a bleeding ulcer. He was just trying to get sympathy and change the subject from him getting a job. He would grab his abdomen, cry out, and double over, supposedly in pain. Then he would go to the bathroom. Later, he would drag me in to triumphantly show me the "blood" in the toilet, to prove he was right. That worked once. Then I saw the red drops on the counter, the stains on his fingers, and my mom's food coloring bottle in his pocket. I told him he was a hypochondriac and needed psychological help. He couldn't keep faking illnesses to get out of working. He had to get a job! He raged that all the nagging was what gave him the ulcer in the first place! "You don't have an ulcer!" I shouted and flushed the toilet. The bowl was stained red. Now I had to clean it and get him to leave before he woke my whole family up. He refused to admit using the food dye, but why else was it in his pocket? Besides, blood doesn't stain like that. 14, 17, 24, 27

I began pleading exhaustion and headaches when he picked me up from work. I was exhausted and thinking about John did give me a headache, so it wasn't really lying. At first, he protested, saying he wanted to party with me and have some "loving." But we soon fell into a new routine. He would take me home after work, except on the nights I got paid. On those nights, he would greet me with a strong drink he had mixed just for me, out of the goodness of his own heart. Sometimes, I would see the undissolved powder of the pills he had put in it. I spilled those drinks before I could drink them. He would claim he was going to give me special treatment because I worked so hard. I always said I just wanted to go home, but he would insist on taking me to his parent's house. There was a movie on HBO that he knew I would love or some other excuse. No amount of pleading or protesting on my part would deter him. After we had been there a while, he would sneak out and do something to his car so it wouldn't start, usually when I was in the bathroom. Later, he would pretend to be so very nice and take me home, but the car would not cooperate. He would pretend to be puzzled and fiddle around with the engine. I would end up spending the night. The next morning, he would stop at the bank so I could cash my check. He always went to the drive-through so he got the tube first. He would take out the money he wanted and give me what little was left. My arguments that it was my money and I needed it fell on deaf ears. He usually took half or more of what I made. When that was gone, we spent what I had left. It never lasted until the next payday. 1, 12, 13, 18, 22, 23, 25

Then somehow, it was *my* fault that he had to go steal something to sell to get us by! Getting a job like a normal person was not a solution he thought of. He stole a lot of HBO units off people's roofs. His family turned a blind eye to his never-ending supply of units and helped him find people who would buy them from him. No matter how much money he had, it was gone in a few days. He was spending more and more on the prescriptions. He had changed doctors so many times I lost count. He stole a prescription pad from one doctor and practiced his signature. He memorized the special number the doctor is assigned to prove the prescription came from him.

By now, John was also on his third set of friends since I had met him. People usually either took an instant dislike to him or were totally charmed when they first met John. Then when their things started disappearing or he bummed money off them too much, it went sour. He didn't care, he made a new friend every week. He used people. Everyone was just someone to steal from or sell stolen goods to. I was extremely uncomfortable with all the theft. I refused to be a part of it. Which, of course, only made him more determined to involve me. He would stop at a house in the middle of the night and say he had to talk to someone. I would wait in the car. A little later, he'd come tearing down the street and throw the stolen goods in the back and race away. Or he would insist that I go with him to meet a new friend and it turned out he was installing an HBO unit for them that day. Then he told me I was an accessory and would be prosecuted too, if he were caught. That scared me since he seemed to always get his way in court. 20

After I had figured out his HBO stealing routine, I had snuck out of his car and run home. A couple of times, I hid in alleys behind giant Dumpsters while he cruised around looking for me. He had been furious that I wasn't there and alternated between calling for me all sweet and yelling threats. Finally, he gave up and went home. I walked home, thankful that he wasn't waiting for me. The next day, he demanded to know what happened to me and why I left. I told him I would not be his lookout or help him steal. It became a challenge for him to try and involve me. He was becoming more and more obsessive about things. 13

That's why he rigged his car so I had a hard time getting out. He had sold the car his mom bought him for a profit. He now had a station wagon that he bought without repaying his mom what he owed her. He did more than sabotage the engine every other Thursday night. As we continued to fight, especially about his stealing, he made the car into a death trap that I had a hard time escaping from. He took off the handles that rolled the windows up and down and hid all, but his. He kept that one under his seat. He kept all the doors locked, except the driver's door. He unscrewed the lock buttons so only the bare screw stuck up. The little screw that worked the lock only showed about a quarter of an inch and was really hard to get a hold of. He fixed all the doors so they only opened from the outside. This was all calculated to keep me under his control. If we were in the car, I could not get out unless I took his window crank from under his seat, rolled down my window, pulled the lock screw up, reached outside the window, and opened the door from the outside, all while he held me down and kept me from leaving! I told him he had made the car a death trap. That if we were in an accident and his door was blocked, I would be unable to escape. He replied, "Don't you want to die with me? How could you want to live if I was gone? You must not love me anymore!" More emotional blackmail! He was very good at it. He did all that to his car to keep me from leaving while he was stealing stuff. When he left to steal, he took the window crank with him. He always said he was just going to talk to someone, like I didn't know what he was up to. 17, 23

He was obsessed with the idea of making his dog, Jinx, a father. He snuck neighbor dogs out of their yards and tried to make Jinx mount them. Who knows if he even picked female dogs! He was so stupid. He didn't know anything about dogs going into heat and not being attracted if the female wasn't in heat. He got really mad at Jinx one night and kicked him. I tried to make him stop. He turned on me. His eyes were wild and black, all pupils from the drugs. He was really high on codeine and alcohol. He grabbed one of the rabbits out of the cage. "You want to boss me?" he screamed. "You want to be in charge?" He strangled that bunny right in front of me, choking and shaking it. I will never forget how horrible it was to watch. I couldn't stop him. He threw it at me and tossed the little neighbor dog over the fence. "That's what happens when you're in charge!" he snarled before stomping into his house. I stayed outside, shaking and petting Jinx. Then he came out crying and said, "Look what you made me do!" He pointed at the bunny on the ground next to me. "I feel so bad. I need you to hold me and say it will be all right." I helped him bury the rabbit after he calmed down. I felt like I was burying the last bit of my sanity. John backed off the pressure about me helping him to steal. He promised to get a job, but in the same breath complained that it was just so hard for him with all his health problems. No one really understood how hard it was for him, he said. I suggested that getting off drugs and alcohol would help him feel better. He exploded. "See that right there proves you don't know anything! It's the only thing that keeps me going. I'm not that bad anyway! You drink a lot too! Maybe you are an alcoholic! How can you point a finger at me when you are just as bad?" He was convinced I was against him. 15, 19, 21

I was exhausted. Between the fights, working sixty hours a week, and trying to keep up with all the animals, it was too much. We had given away the one chicken that survived, but still had the ferret, bunnies at both houses, and all the hamsters at my house. I couldn't keep up with everything. I knew I had to make a decision. I had made a terrible mistake and was paying dearly for it. The question now was, how long was I going to take it? I hadn't really allowed myself to think seriously about a future outside of John. It had taken all my energy just getting through the drama of each day. There had never been time for much reflection. And when I had tried to implement a change, I had met so much resistance, that I ended up dropping it. So I just bounced from one reaction to another based on what was happening with John. I had no self-esteem anymore and very little ambition. I was terrified to leave and terrified to stay. I felt like I could take the "I told you so" from family and friends now. But I knew I wouldn't be able to withstand John's constant pestering if I tried to leave him. I thought back to the year before when he had called Chloe. 4

He had somehow found out what town she lived in. At 3:00 a.m., I watched while he sweet-talked an operator into giving him Chloe's unpublished, unlisted phone number. She could have lost her job for doing it. I was amazed at his ability to charm people into getting whatever he wanted. I remember how cautious Chloe sounded on the phone. I had chalked it up to her being woken up in the middle of the night. Now I realized she had been terrified. She probably moved the next day. He had bragged to me that he could find anyone, anywhere, anytime. He talked to Chloe about her job and where she was living now. He was trying to get information from her, but she was on guard and gave vague answers. Then he mentioned her little sister and said maybe he would go by and pay her a visit. I didn't understand it at the time, but that was a veiled threat. I would receive a similar threat to my little sister later. [19, 20, 25]

So I felt stuck and powerless. I was depressed that I had chosen so badly. I felt I had gotten what I deserved for all the guys I had hurt in the past, even though it had been unintentional. Right in the middle of my turmoil and private struggle, John unknowingly ripped the wool off my eyes and forever ended any feelings of love I might still have had for him.

It happened on a Thursday night in early March. It was payday for me, so we were at his parent's house. I had started watching to try and catch him messing with the car. I had even gone so far as to accuse him of doing something to the car so it wouldn't start. He, of course, denied it. He turned on the charm that I saw right through, saying it was just a weird coincidence, that the car seemed to have a mind of its own and he couldn't help it. A couple times, I snuck out to walk home. He had chased me down in his car that now miraculously started, demanding that I come back. This time, I went straight to the front door when I came out of the bathroom. I peeked through the little window on the door and saw John messing with something under the hood. I opened the door and said, "You better get that car started right now. I'm getting my purse and you are taking me home!" I slammed the door and went to get my purse from the living room. I came back and peeked out again. The hood was still up. John was right in front of the door with his back to it. He slammed his head hard, straight back into the mailbox. Then he lay down on the driveway, called my name, and started jerking around like he was having a seizure. He had claimed to be epileptic after he was supposedly attacked by Mark and his friends with a baseball bat. Standing there, peeking through the drapes, I flashed back to Tom's truck the night Mark hit John. I remember Mark cussing and yelling, my mom yelling, me leaning across Tom's girlfriend, telling Tom to go. Then turning around and seeing John. He had been hunched over toward the dash. All I had focused on was the blood. Now I realized that if Mark had really hit John as he stood outside the truck, the force of the blow would have slammed John's head into me or back into the back window. It would not have forced him forward like he had been sitting. John had smashed his own face into the dash when everyone was distracted. Mom had grabbed Mark's arm just like they said. I had blocked Tom and his girlfriend's view. No one had seen it. John had nearly gotten away with putting my brother in jail for something he did *not* do! 24, 25

Meanwhile, John had stopped twitching and called for me again, louder this time. Then he started jerking around. I opened the door and said, "Show's over. Take me home." He acted all disoriented and confused, still pretending. He "found" the blood on the driveway and made a big show of discovering that it came from his head. He claimed he must have had a seizure. He said he needed stitches. Since I wasn't sure yet just how I was going to use my revelation, I played along that night. He was in his element, telling his story, charming the nurses. I walked home from the hospital and sat up the rest of the night, thinking, remembering, and deciding. I told John the next day that I had some decisions to make. I was unhappy and not sure what to do about it. I asked him to give me the weekend to think. No phone calls, no coming over. Oddly, he agreed without argument. I don't know if he saw me looking through the window and knew he was busted, but he could tell something was bothering me.

I called my friend, Shelley. We hadn't talked for a long time. I asked if she wanted to hang out that weekend. We made plans to see a movie and have her spend the night on Friday. After the movie, Shelley's boyfriend showed up at her house with another guy, Paul. They wanted to go four-wheeling for a little bit. So we all crammed into the cab of his truck and drove out to the desert. We didn't stay long. When they dropped us off at Shelley's, Paul asked for my phone number. I said I was in the process of breaking up with my boyfriend and wasn't available yet. If it worked out, I would have Shelley pass my number on to him through her boyfriend. "Process, huh?" he grinned and said, "Sounds complicated." He seemed like a nice guy and didn't try to kiss me or anything. Shelley and I went back to my house to spend the night. We talked until about 1:30 a.m. I didn't reveal what I had recently discovered. I just let her know I was really unhappy. It felt so good to be with a friend who just accepted me and made no demands. We were sleeping on the sofa bed in the guest room, just across the hall from my room.

I woke up later to a strange flickering light and a noise. It was after 3:00 a.m. John was walking down the hall, flicking on his lighter, and looking around. He found me and demanded that I get up. I said, "No, go away. I'm supposed to get the weekend to myself." Then I saw that he had my hamster in his other hand. I didn't want to wake Shelley up. I recognized that look in his eyes. I got up and he started down the hall. I followed him, asking quietly for my hamster. He was a grey teddy bear with really fluffy fur. I loved him! "Please, John, let me put him back in his cage!" I begged. John was holding him really tightly. I could see Teddy struggling. If he bit John, it would be bad. John had gone to the front door. He had left it open, letting all the cold air in. "John, please! Give him to me!" I hissed. He bent down and let go of Teddy. I started to lean over to scoop him up, but John stood up rapidly. He slammed his shoulder into my stomach, wrapped his arms around my legs, and finished standing. Before I knew it, he was running down our walkway with me. He threw me in the car, jumped in, and drove away. He drove with one hand and was punching me in the face with the other. His car door had been open, the engine running. He had planned this! 10, 19, 23, 26

He was screaming at me. I was so scared and shocked, I didn't hear everything. Some words got through, like "whore, slut, lesbian!" I stayed lying on the seat and kicked with all my might. I know I got him in the head a couple of times and a few good kicks to his ribs. He stopped punching and started trying to deflect my kicks. I screamed at the top of my lungs until I ran out of breath. I have no idea how we didn't wreck with him racing down the street while all this happened. He stopped at the end of the block and I started screaming again. He yelled at me to shut up, but I kept screaming, so he drove off. That went on for some time. He would stop to try and talk to me, but I would just scream for help, so he would drive off again. A cop went past once and I screamed as loud as I could, but he never even looked at us. Finally, I demanded to go home. John refused, "Not until we talk." 5, 7, 8, 12, 23

"There is nothing to talk about!" I yelled.

"You need to wash your face first. I can't talk to you until you do," he said.

"What the hell are you talking about?" I screamed at him. Then I flipped the visor down. In the mirror, I could see blood all over the bottom half of my face. I felt so cold inside. He had given me a bloody nose and split my bottom lip open so far the insides were coming out!

"Take me home now, you asshole!" I began to scream again, over and over. "I'll have you in jail for this! How dare you hit me!" He explained that he wouldn't go to jail because I had simply hit my face on the dash when he had to brake suddenly. A cat had run across the road and I never wore my seat belt. "There's no blood on the dash, genius!" I sneered. Then he produced a syringe with blood in it. God only knows where that came from! He squirted the blood on the dash. "It won't match my blood type, stupid!" I yelled. "It doesn't need to. No one will see

THE PITS OF HELL
a need to test it. We just avoided a cat, and if you would wear your seat belt like I keep telling you to, this wouldn't have happened!" He sounded so calm, so reasonable. I knew the cops would believe him. Damn it, they always did! We argued until about 5:00 a.m. Finally, he stopped at his parent's house and brought me a wet washcloth. I dabbed at my face without a word. He didn't even apologize. He said if I hadn't cheated on him, he wouldn't have to punish me. "Cheat on you with whom?" I asked. "That girl in your bed," he replied. "All we did was talk and sleep, you idiot! There was eighteen inches of space between us!" I was dumbfounded. 13, 21, 24

He dropped me off in front of my parent's house and said he'd call me later when I had calmed down. "Don't bother, you dickhead!" I said, "We are done! You made the decision for me. I never want to see you again!" I stomped in the house and collapsed on the bed. Later, when Shelley woke up, I told her to give my phone number to Paul. Maybe I should have waited, but I was angry and not thinking. I kept my lip sucked in so she wouldn't see and said nothing about what had happened. She apparently hadn't noticed me missing during the night. Shelley had an ex-boyfriend who had beat her up, so I knew she would understand. But I was ashamed and not ready to talk about it yet. 27

I told Mom if John called to just hang up on him. "Are you guys fighting again?" she asked. "No, we're through." I said. It was getting close to Mark's birthday. I felt this was a great gift, to have John out of our lives. I mostly stayed to myself Saturday and Sunday. I kept my lip pulled in so no one would see. The last thing we needed was for Mark to go after John for hitting me. John called Saturday afternoon, but was hung up on. He called over a dozen times. I refused to talk to him. He called me at work Sunday night, but I just kept hanging up. The ladies I worked with were horrified at my lip and praised me for dumping him. No one there liked John anyway. 9

I told the guy who answered the phone that I wouldn't talk to John, so to just hang up on him. Later that night, the buzzer for the back door rang. The supervisor went to check and came back with a huge flower arrangement for me. John had brought it. Now she felt sorry for him. "He looked so sad and sincere!" she said. "Maybe you should forgive him."

"Are you out of your mind? Look at what he did to me!" I said. Then I saw the card stuck in the flowers. "Dear Edith, I hope you are better and can come home soon. Love, Agnes."

"Look," I said. "He stole these flowers from some little old lady in the hospital! There are no florists open at 11:00 at night!" What a dick he was! Everything he ever gave me was bought by someone else or he stole it! He called over a dozen times that night. 13

The next day, he gave a different name so my sister called me to the phone. As soon as I heard his voice, I hung up. He tried the same trick at work that night. I told them I was refusing all calls. Later that week, he would call my parents, and when we hung up, he wouldn't. This kept the line open and we couldn't call out. Mom would have to go to the neighbor's and explain the situation to an operator, who would then disconnect the line. It was a pain.

Paul called early in the week and asked me out for Friday night. I said yes. I was nervous and excited at the same time. It had been so long since I had done anything that didn't revolve around John's moods. I didn't know what to wear or even how to pick out my own clothes. John had dictated that too. The only new clothes I had were the sweats Mom gave me at Christmas. I needed to go shopping, but with who? I had discovered that most of my friends had moved on. They were busy with college or jobs during the day while I worked at night. I wasn't going to drive myself and I did not want to go with Mom. My lip still looked bad, so I was avoiding her as much as possible. I ended up just choosing pants and a top I hadn't worn in a long time, nothing fancy. 18

During that first week, I had time to just think. A lot of stuff came back to me that I had either ignored, denied, or repressed. It sickened me just how far I had sunk. I was really out of shape, but didn't want to go running for fear John would show up. I didn't want to get thrown into the death trap again. It was too cold to swim, so I exercised in my room while I remembered. I came to the conclusion that John had cheated on me repeatedly, probably our whole relationship. The times he would stop during sex and say I was "loose" corresponded with times that different people had told me of seeing him with someone else. His friends would start to mention something they had done with John and he would silence them with a look. It was his guilty conscience that caused him to accuse me. Or maybe it was just perverse cruelty on his part. I hadn't wanted to believe it, so I didn't.

Random things popped into my head as I worked out. Like the time I was spending the night at his house and he woke me up at 3:00 a.m. He had heated pizza in the microwave for me. Apparently, he thought I wanted to be woken up out of a sound sleep after a ten-hour shift to eat pizza! I tried to nicely decline, thanking him sweetly. I explained that I was really tired and just wanted to sleep. I saw the look in his eyes just in time and turned my head. He smashed burning hot pizza into the side of my head, yelling that no one ever appreciated all the nice thoughtful things he did for them. My scalp blistered in a few places and it took a while to get all the cheese out of my hair. I was thankful that I had turned my head or my face would have been burned. The next day, he drove me to the bank and took most of my money like nothing had ever happened. 1, 11, 16, 18, 21

He often fixed food in the middle of the night. His mom would get so mad at him for ruining her Teflon skillets by cooking eggs in them. He always used a fork to stir them around with, and it tore the coating up terribly. I don't know how many platefuls of eggs with Teflon bits in them I choked down. If he decided to cook, there was no stopping him. It didn't matter if you were hungry. No amount of begging him to use a spatula or offering to cook for him deterred him from ruining the pans. He delighted in knowing his mom would be mad, it seemed. 18

It was the same way with his disgusting habit of hocking loogies and spitting them in the trash cans. It was so gross! His mom complained about stuff being stuck to the trash can from it. She asked him to stop, but he just did it more. He could be very spiteful and mean-spirited.

I hated his habit of drumming on everything, including me. He said he couldn't help it, the music took over him. He would be drumming in the car, on the steering wheel, the dash, my leg. His fingers were long and he kind of snapped them as he made contact. It really stung. I would cry out and move my leg. I asked him to stop because it hurt. "Oh, that didn't hurt. You're just a big baby! You gotta get into the music!" he'd say and turn it up louder. I would answer, "It did hurt," and move away. Then he grabbed hold of my leg and pulled me back close to him. "You sit close to me or you don't ride with me!" he said. If I said the music was too loud, he'd turn it up louder. He said you couldn't hear it right unless it was loud. I don't think he could hear anything right because he was deaf! 1, 12

During that first week apart, I reexamined my last two babysitting jobs. John had suddenly decided to take me to the movies one night. There was a horror movie playing about a babysitter getting prank calls to check the children. It turned out the killer was in the house, calling from upstairs. The movie freaked me out even though I hadn't done any sitting lately. Then a few days later, John's newest doctor called and asked me to watch his kids. His regular sitter was sick and John had recommended me. I accepted. He was paying more than my usual fee since it was short notice. John drove me and dropped me off. The two kids were ready for bed and just needed a story first. I promised that John wouldn't be there to distract me. After the parents left, John started prank calling. He changed his voice, telling me to check the children. I figured out it was him pretty quickly, but it still scared me. The doctor had a big two-story house like in the movie. I felt sure that John had set me up. I just didn't know why he would do that. He called later and I told him I didn't like being scared like that. He laughed and said to lighten up. He said I didn't have a sense of humor. He totally disregarded my feelings. 1, 12

When John saw how much money I made watching the doctor's kids, he volunteered us to watch his nieces on New Year's Eve. I loved those little girls! They were adorable and we got along well. The younger one had a bad cough and was on a prescription for it. When Carla was giving me the directions for the cough syrup, I noticed it had codeine in it. I asked about that. She said codeine helps with coughs and to be careful with it. The syrup was expensive. She had just bought it the day before. 18, 22

We played with the girls until about 10:00 p.m. They were allowed to stay up later than usual that night. John was drinking as always. At bedtime, I went to get the cough syrup for her last dose. The bottle was on the bathroom sink instead of in the medicine cupboard where Carla had put it. It was much lighter when I picked it up. I looked closely at the bottle. It was nearly empty! "John!" I called, "Come here! What happened to this?" I asked. He had been in the bathroom last. He denied touching it. His eyes were a dead giveaway that he was high on codeine. I had seen him like this plenty of times. I knew he had drunk almost all of his poor sick niece's cough syrup. If that didn't prove he was an addict, I don't know what would! John suggested maybe I had spilled it. "Of course I didn't spill it!" I said. "I found it like this. Your sister put it away and it was here on the sink when I came in. Admit it, you drank her medicine!" He blew up at me. I didn't want to fight in front of the girls, so I let it go at the time. 14, 19, 21, 24

When Carla and her boyfriend came home, she was really upset about the cough medicine. There wasn't enough for all of the next day's doses and no pharmacies were open since it was New Year's Day. I felt badly that it had happened on my watch. I told Carla she didn't have to pay me for sitting. I said she should use the money to get a refill. That pissed off John. He demanded to get paid. After all, he claimed he had worked babysitting and he wasn't the one who had spilled it all! That did it! I turned on him and hissed, "I didn't spill it! You drank it!" Carla was really mad, but John stuck to his story. It was all my fault in his eyes. He tried so hard and everyone just harped on him. It was so unfair, etc. We left and Carla never had me sit for her again. I gave up hope of John ever admitting his addictions and getting help. 22, 24

Something I had repressed came back to me when I was switching buses on Thursday. I always switched buses at the same stop on the way to work. That day John was waiting and tried to talk to me. He offered to give me a ride to work. I had about fifteen minutes before the next bus showed up. I tried ignoring him, but he wouldn't go away. I told him to leave. Other people were waiting for the bus and a guy spoke up and suggested John listen to me and just go. He pounced on that. "Oh, so you are fucking this guy now, huh? I always knew you were a slut, whore. You weren't a virgin when we met! Do they form a line on the bus and take turns until your stop comes up?" he screamed. I was humiliated at all his language. I rode the bus with most of these people every day! The guy said he was going into the store to call the cops and John finally left. While I was sitting there with my face burning in shame, another incident flooded my mind. 7, 8, 24

It had been the previous fall right before Thanksgiving. John had been really working the "return shoplifted goods for money" thing hard. He wanted me to go to K-Mart with him because he had been there too many times. I refused. He bugged me about it day after day. That day, he offered me a ride to work, but left really early. I asked what was up. He said it was a surprise. Surprise! The surprise was he took me to K-Mart to return stolen goods. I told him I would not help him with his scam. I am not a good liar and don't like doing it. He got mad and started yelling. "I'm doing this for you! So I can get you a super nice Christmas gift! Don't you care about anything?" His logic only made sense to him. Besides, any money he had in November would be spent on pills before Christmas came around. 13, 16, 21, 26

He was pulling on my arm, trying to drag me into the store. I braced my feet and screamed "No!" as loud as I could over and over. I finally broke free and ran. He caught up to me, slamming me into a car. "You are going to do this for me!" he screamed in my face. "No, I'm not!" I screamed back. "Even if you get me in the store, I won't say one word at the Customer Service counter. Leave me alone!" He started dragging me again. I managed to break free and ran as fast as I could. I made it out of the parking lot to the road. I decided to walk to the bus stop and go to work even though it was early. I had to cross the freeway. It was a scene from many nightmares I've had before. I'm terrified of heights and having cars whiz past me while crossing the overpass greatly increased my anxiety. But I did it! I had my purse with me, but hadn't grabbed the stuff I usually took to work. John's mom had given me a kit to make a flower afghan. I was making it for her Christmas present. It gave me something to do on the bus and at work on break. But I wasn't about to go back for it. 23, 25

About a block after I crossed the freeway, a small truck stopped next to me. I didn't look closely at the driver and couldn't tell at first, if it was a man or woman. They asked if I needed a ride. I said, "No, thanks." I kept walking fast, not really looking over. "I heard you screaming in the parking lot. Do you need help?" the driver asked. I got a better look and that's when I saw the child. It was a mom with a kid, no older than two. No way was I going to involve them in this mess. Just as I started to assure her I was fine, John pulled up behind her. He jumped out of his car and ran toward me. "I'm fine, go!" I yelled, starting to run. He caught my hair and dragged me off the sidewalk. There was a tall hedge dividing two lawns. He dragged me through the grass halfway down the length of the hedge. A man and his son stopped and came after John. The lady was still stopped and cars were honking. The man and his son yelled at John to leave me alone. John turned to confront them. I jumped up and took off again. The lady with the toddler said, "Get in, I'll take you wherever you need to go!" But I told her to just go before John hurt her or her child. I ran down the sidewalk, praying a bus would be at the stop when I got there. God answered that prayer. I got on and tried to pay the fare. My hands were shaking so badly, I couldn't count out the change. I finally handed some coins to the driver. He put in the right amount and gave me back the rest. I forgot to ask for a transfer slip, so I had to ask when I was getting off. "You're supposed to get one when you board," the driver said. 14, 23, 25

"I know, I'm sorry," I replied. He stared at me. I had been crying. He gave me the transfer slip. "Are you all right?" he asked.

"No, but there's nothing you can do about it," I said and got off the bus.

I must have looked a fright when I got to work. I was about an hour early. I tried to clean up a little in the bathroom. I couldn't get the grass stains out of my clothes. I sat in the break room, drinking coffee and trying to calm down. When my supervisor came in, she commented on how early I was. I told her I had taken an earlier bus because John and I had had a fight. "Well, people fight," she said. Then she saw how pale I was and I was still shaking. "Maybe you should break up with him if you guys fight a lot," she said. *It's not that easy*, I thought and followed her out of the break room. John called work a little later and said he had dumped the afghan flowers out on the road. Then he called and said he had told his mom that I was making it for her. Later, the back door buzzer sounded. When the supervisor came back, she had the bag of flowers with her. "No one was there, just this bag. Does anyone know what's going on?" she asked, looking at me. Of course, everyone knew that I worked on those flowers at break every night. "Thank you," I said. "I left them in John's car." No one said anything. They gave me space and waited to see if I wanted to talk. I didn't. John called later to see if I had the bag. "Stop calling! I'm going to get in trouble," I told him.

"We have to talk!" he insisted.

"Not when I'm working. I can't keep getting phone calls," I explained.

"But you have to listen to me. You make me crazy! I don't know what I'll do!" he cried.

"I make *you* crazy? You make me *crazy*! I can't talk now. I'm at work. You know that thing *grownups* do to earn money! Don't call again. We can talk tomorrow." I hung up on him. [9, 10, 20, 26, 27]

My friend, Kari, said she'd drive me home that night. John was waiting in the parking lot. He tried to talk me into getting in his car. Kari rang the buzzer and told the guy who answered to call the cops. John left, but he showed up at my house after Kari dropped me off. We argued for what seemed like hours. He could get me so turned around. Finally, he said I should be nice to him. "I'm going to court tomorrow. You might want to be nice to me or things won't go well for your brother!" Damn! I hated how smug he got. I forgave him and repressed the whole ugly incident until now: triggered by another ugly scene at the bus stop. [4, 20]

Looking back, it seemed so violent, but I had rationalized that he hadn't actually hit me. I'm sure he was going to kick me when the guys stopped him. But since he didn't, I told myself it wasn't that bad. I was probably overreacting. Besides, I had to keep him happy or he would send Mark to prison.

Friday came and I nervously got ready for my date with Paul. He came in, met my parents and two little sisters. When we got to his car, he said he hadn't eaten and asked where I wanted to go. It had been so long since anyone asked me what I wanted to do! I couldn't think! "You choose," I told him. He stopped at a fast-food place, but I didn't order any food. I was so nervous, I was afraid I'd get sick. Paul explained that he hadn't been in Phoenix very long. He had been engaged, and when his fiancée broke up with him, he moved here for a fresh start. He and Shelley's boyfriend were childhood friends. He had told him Phoenix was nice. So he moved. He had an entry level job at a computer firm and a studio apartment. "I don't have a lot of spending money because I'm trying to save up. But there are lots of things we can do that don't cost a lot, if you don't mind," he said. I was thinking, *A guy with a job and a bank account! What a difference for a change!*

We decided to go to his place to eat. I sat at the table watching him eat his burger and fries. He offered me some fries. I munched a few. I felt so uncomfortable. I would not take my sweater off. He opened us each a beer, then we played chess. I beat him two out of three games. "Not going to give a guy a break on his birthday, huh?" he teased. I blushed really red. "Sorry, I didn't know. Happy birthday," I said. Paul stood up to put the chess game away and I flinched. I couldn't help it. He came around and slowly took my hands. He pulled me up and looked closely at me. Then he touched my bottom lip. It was healing, but there was still evidence of John's fist.

"He did that to you?" Paul asked quietly. "Yes," I said. I couldn't look him in the eye. He moved his hand to my chin and raised my face a little. "Does it hurt?" he asked. "Not much anymore," I replied. Then he asked if he could kiss me. *Asked!* I nodded, blushing furiously, heart pounding. He was very gentle and sweet. He didn't try to do anything else, just kissed me. He pulled away some and asked again if my lip hurt. I couldn't talk just then, so I shook my head. He smiled. I could feel him smiling. He kissed me again. Then he stepped back and said, "Promise me you won't go back to that guy."

"I won't," I assured him. "I hate him!"

He suggested I take my sweater off for the second time. For some reason, I just felt naked without it on. I don't know why. The shirt I was wearing wasn't revealing. I let him help me slip out of it. We sat on his bed and he turned on the TV. He asked what I wanted to watch. I had no idea what shows were even on anymore. Other than an occasional HBO movie, TV hadn't existed in Johnland where I had spent the last year and a half. "It's your birthday, you pick," I told him. We watched for a while with me sitting stiffly, perfectly straight next to him. Paul reached up to touch my hair, and damn it, I flinched again. He got this really sad look on his face. "How many times has he hurt you?" he asked. "Hurt me or hit me?" I tried to clarify. He took a deep breath and slowly released it. Then he gently cradled my face with his hands and looked in my eyes. "I will never intentionally hurt you or ever hit you," he said. "I want you to know that, right now." I felt like I was going to cry. Then he grinned and said, "Hey! You never gave me a birthday kiss!"

"What? I did!" I protested.

"No, that was a lip-healing kiss from me to you," he teased. And he asked again if he could kiss me.

We kissed for quite a while. I realized we were now lying back on his bed with our feet dangling off the end. He sat up and said his feet were falling asleep. He asked if we could move up to lie completely on the bed. He must have seen the pure panic on my face. "I won't try anything," he promised. So we scooched up and started kissing again. He was a really good kisser. John had been so demanding and rough. I felt like I could kiss Paul forever. He never tried to lie on top of me. We mostly stayed on our sides. At one point, he turned and took me with him, so I was on top of him. He never stopped kissing me, so I relaxed. Then his hand moved on my back. As it touched my bra strap, I froze. "I'm sorry," we both said at the same time. I sat up fast and moved away. "I can't have sex with you, not even for your birthday. I know I didn't get you anything, but I can't. I'm sorry, I just can't do that!" I was rambling. "Whoa, slow down. It's okay," he said. "I don't expect you to have sex with me, birthday or not." I felt like an idiot! I just wanted my sweater back, like Linus and his stupid blanket!

Paul handed me my sweater and watched me put it on. I tied it tight around my waist. Then he hugged me. He held me for a long time. Finally, he noticed the time. "Wow! It's almost 1:00! I better get you home," he said. We talked a little on the way home. I was praying John wouldn't be there to start trouble. Paul walked me to the door. He asked if I'd like to do something next weekend. "Maybe we could have a picnic at the park?" he suggested. I thought that sounded great!

I went asleep happy and hopeful for the first time in a very long time. Then at 3:00 a.m., John put his fist through my window and tried to choke me. He got all cut up. I was hysterical. I told him to leave and bleed to death somewhere else. He was, as usual, very drunk and high. He threatened to kill himself if I didn't come out and talk to him. "Good!" I hissed. "Then all my problems will be solved, jerk!" He wouldn't leave until I threatened to get my dad. I told him Dad would call the cops about the window. I didn't even tell Dad about it for a long time. It was one small triangular piece of glass broken out. I cut some cardboard and put it in to keep out the cold. I wanted to save some money to have it fixed myself. Looking back, I guess I should have woke my parents up and let them call the police. Maybe things would have turned out differently. 7, 14, 16, 20, 27

Saturday, I walked a few blocks to a shopping center. It had small clothes shop. I bought a really pretty blouse to wear for the picnic with Paul. It felt good to get something for myself. I continued to hang up on John without giving him a chance to mess with my head. I didn't care about him one bit, not his cut arm, his hurt feelings, anything he had to say. Every time I replayed him smashing his head into the mailbox, I was mad at myself for being so stupid. I felt miserable about all the trouble Mark and my family had gone through because of my relationship with John. I felt that I could resist him and stay strong as long as I didn't listen to him. Surely, he would get tired and go away.

Monday afternoon, when he called, I heard him say, "Don't hang up. It's about Mark!" My hand froze halfway.

Slowly, I pulled the receiver back to my ear. Maybe I had heard wrong. "What?" I demanded. Then he proceeded to inform me that he had been talking to his lawyer. He had a six-month grace period in which to refile the original assault charges, if Mark started bugging him again. "He never did anything in the first place!" I screamed into the phone. "Maybe not, but I'm pretty sure he drove past my house last night," John replied. He was so calm and in control. "So unless you want your precious Marky to go to prison, you'll get back together with me!" He was so smug! How I hated him at that moment! I couldn't think. I needed time, so I said, "Don't call me again until Wednesday. I will give you an answer then."

"Fine," he crooned, "talk to you Wednesday, babe. Have a nice night at work!" [20, 25]

As I hung up, my head was spinning. What could I do? I hadn't foreseen this move. Mark was getting married in June. It was now the middle of March. I had held my ground for ten days. Now John had tipped the balance of power back in his favor. The grace period would not be up until July 17. I had to stop John from ruining Mark's wedding and his life! But to get back together with him was intolerable! After having a date with a guy who was sweet and respectful, to go back to John made me sick. The next two days, I went round and round in my head, trying out different scenarios and schemes to get the upper hand and protect Mark. I couldn't go to the cops. They always believed John. I didn't say anything to my family or friends. I didn't want to involve them in case things went badly. Besides, I felt I had to fix this mess myself. It was *my* mess. I owed it to Mark to protect him from John's madness.

By Wednesday, a plan had formed in my mind. John called and said, "So what do you think? Do I call my lawyer and have Marky picked up again or have you come to your senses?" I said, "Things cannot be the same as before. You *have* to get a real job. If you want me back, you have to prove it. I need to see that you are growing up. Understand?"

"Sure, babe, whatever you want!" he said so sweetly. I had to go to work, so I said, "Call me tomorrow. We can discuss it further." He honored this demand, letting me think I was in control. I had decided that I was done proving things to John. He was going to have to win me back. Maybe he would decide I wasn't worth it and leave me alone.

Paul called Thursday on his lunch to see what time to pick me up on Saturday. In all the turmoil about John, I had forgotten our picnic date! That's the way it was with John. He wasn't just a part of my life, he became my whole life, like it or not. I felt horrible. I knew I couldn't keep Paul dangling while I worked on getting rid of John. I was sure John was going to be around until at least the middle of July, when the grace period was up. And who knew what drama he would come up with before then. Paul was so nice! He was like a dream come true and John was a nightmare that I couldn't wake up from. But Mark's fate hung in the balance. I had to stay strong and tough this out. I told Paul I couldn't go Saturday. I was getting back together with John. My throat was so tight. My heart was breaking. I knew if I tried to explain it, I would break down and cry. I couldn't risk involving Paul. John would make it his mission to destroy him!

So I let him think that I just couldn't live without John and wanted him back. He was tremendously hurt. "You promised to stay away from him! He's going to hurt you again!" he protested. I just said, "Sorry," and hung up. I hoped Paul would find a really nice girl and be happy. I didn't deserve another chance with him, even though I didn't plan on being with John for much longer. 13, 18, 25, 27

Friday night, John picked me up. I told him I wanted to go dancing at a nice place. He took me to a disco club. He bought me a mixed drink without complaint. He was being so nice, I was nervous. I spilled the drink before even taking a sip. The glass was really wet from condensation and it dropped out of my hand. I paid for the replacement since I felt badly about the waste. We danced and talked. I told him he really hadn't been treating me well the past few months. "You're going to be twenty-one in August. It is time to grow up," I said. "We are only together conditionally. You are on probation with me." I tried to put it in terms I thought he would understand. "If you really want us to work, you have to get a job and stop all this drama and trouble making. We have to get an apartment of our own. No more fighting at our parents' houses in the wee hours of the morning." He agreed to all my terms without argument. I was surprised. Maybe this breakup was really good. Maybe he is willing to change, I thought. I was wrong. He was merely biding his time, letting me set my own trap. I was playing right into his hands without realizing it. 13

I figured he would balk at getting a job or, at least, stall for a while. Then he would make a dramatic show of dumping me since I had hurt his pride by breaking up with him. When he told me about him and Chloe getting back together, he claimed they stayed together for two weeks before he dumped her. I thought I could hold on until July 17. After all, we had been together for over a year and a half. Not all of it had been so bad, had it? What a stupid, naïve idiot I was!

I realized John was putting drugs in my drinks again. We would be out at a club, and the next thing I knew, we would be in the back of his car, naked. It would be hours later. I had no idea how long he had been having sex with me while I was out. He said it was the best I had ever been in bed! I knew it wasn't the codeine he was grinding up and putting in my drink, nor was I drinking so much that I passed out from alcohol. It made me nauseous and gave me a terrible headache. I had no memory of most of the night. John always said I was crazy and just making it up. He would tell me what we had supposedly done and said. Who knew if it was true or not? I didn't trust his version of events, but at least I wasn't having to consciously endure sex with him. I let it go. 12, 18, 25

He got a job at a new hospital that had just opened. Then in early April, we went apartment hunting. Most of the ones we could afford were dumps. Finally, we found a nice apartment in a medium-sized complex just off the freeway. It was U-shaped with a pool and barbeques in the courtyard and clean. The apartment was on the second floor close to the pool and not far from the laundry room. John and Barb, the manager, hit it off right away. We signed a six-month lease on a one bedroom with a big closet. I wasn't planning on being there for six months, but I figured John would sweet-talk his way out of the lease, like he did everything else.

My family was extremely upset at the turn of events. John's family was ecstatic! His mom said she knew I was good for him. Here he was working full-time, getting a place of his own, growing up to be something! His dad hugged and kissed me. They were so happy to have him move out, they gave him the double bed from Jeff's old room and the furniture from John's room. He said we could put the corner group in the living room since neither one of us had anything besides bedroom furniture. I left my twin bed at home.

Our move-in day was in the middle of April. As I was in my room packing, Mom came in. "I wish you would not do this!" she said. "He's not good for you. I don't understand why you went back to him. Please don't move in with him!" It was hard to maintain my composure. I couldn't face Mom, so I kept my head down and continued to put books in a box. "I have to do it," I said.

"No, you don't!" she countered.

"Yes, I do. I have to," I emphasized. Finally, she sighed and said if I ever needed to, I could always come home, no questions asked. I teared up and almost broke down at that. It was a good thing Mom had left the room. I decided against bringing my pets to the apartment. Mom said they could stay. "He'll probably just be mean to them anyway," she said. *You have no idea!* I thought.

John got into a fight with his mom about the pillows he was taking from their house. She had bought new ones to fix up Jeff's old room as a guest room. John wasn't happy with his old ones and tried to take the new pillows. As usual, I stood back and let them fight it out. He was high, but not extremely so. I had misgivings about this whole thing already. "You can do this!" I told myself. "It's for Mark. You owe him." Besides, how bad could it get? It would only be for a little while. I could handle it. Oh, how wrong I was! John had lured me into a false sense of security by complying with all my demands. I knew he was going to gloat, make a scene at some point, but I greatly underestimated just how angry he was and how much planning he had been doing. I thought all I had to do was put up with some temper tantrums and him strutting around like a big shot, then suffer through a dramatic, public dumping. Then I would be rid of him. He would have paid me back for hurting him and life would go on. I did not allow myself to think beyond that point. "Just get through the next three months, one day at a time. That's all I have to do," I told myself. I never even made it to July, let alone the seventeenth. In fact, I only lasted six weeks. By that time, I was dead. My body was still functioning, barely, but every shred of emotion, my personality, my very soul had been killed, little by little, by John. He spent that six weeks systematically beating, torturing and starving me to death. I lived on coffee, cigarettes, and beer. If I wasn't an alcoholic before we moved in, I certainly was when I moved out. [14,25]

More than one in three women (35.6 percent) and more than one in four men (28.5 percent) in the United States have experienced rape, physical violence, and stalking by an intimate partner in their lifetime.[1]

Females ages eighteen to thirty-four generally experienced the highest rates of intimate partner violence.[2]

PART 2

Descending into the Pits

We moved in on a beautiful, sunny Saturday. It was a nice one-bedroom on the second floor. There was a large walk-in closet. The window in the bedroom overlooked the river rock landscaping below. To the left, looking out that window, you could see the end of the parking lot where our assigned spaces were. We were given two, but I didn't drive or have a car, so we only needed one. They were on the end, just like our apartment. I had calmed down after the fight between John and his mom over the pillows. He said he would arrange the living room and hook up the HBO. He had stolen a unit so he could have movies. That was fine with me; I didn't want my fingerprints on it anyway. I was in the bedroom unpacking my books and arranging them on my shelves. He had brought the majority of the furniture. Besides the bed and corner group for the living room, he had end tables and a small dining room set. I brought the kitchen and bath stuff—all the dishes, silverware, towels, and pots and pans. I had been saving and putting stuff in my hope chest for years. I had brought my wall unit with all my books. John decided it would be best in the bedroom. We each had our own dresser and I had my now nearly empty hope chest tucked in the walk-in closet. This wasn't how I had planned on setting up house for the first time, but, oh well, July 17 wasn't that far away.

The apartment was laid out so that when you walked in the door, the dining area was directly in front of you, with a view straight ahead into the kitchen and the living room to the right. There was a large window overlooking the pool and courtyard below. The walkway outside ended just after our door, so this big window didn't open. I guess they didn't want anyone climbing out and falling two stories. There was another window next to the front door. It went from the floor to the ceiling and was only about twelve inches wide. At the bottom, half the window would slide open for some air flow. The part that opened was about six inches wide and twelve inches high. The window in the bedroom was exactly like this one. The living room and kitchen were separated by a wall about three or four feet long. It formed half of the hall that led to the bedroom. You could circle through the dining area, kitchen, short hall, and back into the living room. The bathroom was on the right going down the hall. That left the bedroom and walk-in. The closet ended before the end of the building. You could see the outside wall of it when looking out the window. I spent a lot of time looking out that window.

So there I was, arranging books, trying to pretend things were normal. Telling myself I could *do* this! I had succeeded with my plan and all I had to do was make it to July 17th. Three months—it wouldn't be so bad. John would be at work during the day and with me working at night, we'd hardly see each other. I was still waiting for John to spring a nasty surprise on me. I figured he would wait until we were settled in and I was off guard. I had vastly underestimated how angry he was or just how evil he could be.

I heard him call me from the living room. "Come here! I need your help with this HBO cable." I really didn't want anything to do with the HBO, but I didn't want him mad either. So I walked down the hall into the living room. He had put the TV against the wall that separated the bathroom and living room. I was focused on heading there and didn't see him. He was pressed against the wall around the corner. When I stepped into the living room, he stepped behind me, grabbed my hair, and jerked me to the floor. Before I had time to think or react, he was putting pressure on my throat with one foot. He reached behind him and pulled out a shotgun. With this smug look on his face, he fished out two shotgun shells from the pocket of his scrubs. Never taking his eyes off me, he loaded both barrels and pressed the shotgun against my head—right between my eyebrows.

He released the pressure on my throat a little and said, "If you ever try to move out of this apartment, I'll kill you. I'll kill your mother, your father, your brother, your sisters, your friends, the people you work with, anyone who tries to help you! Do you understand me?" His voice had built in intensity as he talked. He practically shouted the last words. I didn't blink or even breathe. I just said, "You might as well pull the trigger now." He glared at me for a moment. I lay perfectly still, waiting. Then he got this super smug look on his face, applied more pressure again with his foot, and said, "No, you don't get off that easy. This is a fight to the death. If I have to search the world over a dozen times and it takes me the rest of my life, I'll find you and kill you. You and your whole family. I've only just begun to play with you!" [20]

He pulled his foot away. I took a deep breath and he kicked me in the ribs, hard. The shotgun was still pressed to my head. I will never forget how cold it felt. He hocked up a big loogie, moved the gun, and spit in my face. He knew how disgusted I was at his gross habit. As I scrambled for the bathroom to clean my face, I heard him laugh and say, "The fight is on! Oh yeah, I'm having fun with you now!" I cleaned my face with shaking fingers. I told myself it wasn't so bad. Yeah, my ribs hurt, but I would live. I had to make it for Mark's sake.

When I came out of the bathroom, he said to get my purse. We were going grocery shopping. He bought way too much stuff: steaks, bacon, coffee, cereal, Kool-Aid, and tons of beer. I told him how much we had to spend and that he was going over. He ignored me. When it was all rung up, he had to put stuff back. The store was busy and he was embarrassed that so many people witnessed him not having enough money. I knew better than to say a word.

After we got back and put the groceries away, he started drinking. I realized he had taken a lot of pills. His eyes were almost completely dilated. He turned on the TV and wanted to make Kool-Aid. That was his newest obsession. He drank at least one pitcher of Kool-Aid a day. I had a plastic pitcher that I got out for him. He refused to use it. He dug around in my boxes until he found my crystal pitcher. He insisted things tasted better being poured from the crystal rather than the plastic. "Please be careful with it!" I said. "It was expensive. It's really only for company or special occasions."

"So I'm not *good* enough to use your stuff, huh?" He slammed the pitcher on the counter. It didn't break, but everything jumped. One of the glasses fell over and broke. "Look, see how rough you are with my stuff!" I cried out. "Please use the plastic drinking cups! They are for every day, not the crystal." This became one of many ways John tormented me. He deliberately broke my things. Sometimes, he pretended it was an accident; sometimes, he smiled cruelly and smashed it in front of me. He would say he had talked to his mom about it and the crystal was "cheap junk. That's why it broke so easily." In the end, there was nothing left of that set. The pitcher and all thirty-two glasses had been broken. By the time the last one bit the dust, I didn't care anymore. 25

John had several ongoing methods of torture that he cycled through while we occupied that apartment. The only thing that changed was the order he utilized them in and the intensity of that day's "games." When he broke the first glass, he decided to teach me a lesson about thinking he wasn't good enough. I had to be shown that I was not better than he was. So he told me to go get naked in the bedroom. I obeyed, not really knowing what to expect. Most of our sexual encounters since getting back together had happened while I was out of it. He enjoyed drugging me and experimenting. In a way, this was better for me, I felt. I didn't have to consciously endure his inept attentions, but I also wondered just what he did to me. I had bite marks in intimate places and was usually very sore when I came to.

Now to be conscious somehow seemed ominous. But I was trying not to set him off and make things worse. He came in the room. I was sitting naked on the edge of the bed. "John," I said, "we haven't finished unpacking. Really, we should get things put in order. I have to work tomorrow. Wouldn't it be nice to have everything done?" I had never seen the look on his face before. It was terrifying! I wanted desperately to dissuade him from continuing, but I also didn't want his temper to explode. "Stand up!" he demanded. I did and that's when I saw the glass in his hand. Not a little piece of the glass, but the bottom and what was left of the sides. He circled me slowly, breathing deeply.

Then he stopped in front of me and held up the broken glass. The sun coming in the window behind him glinted off the sharp edges as he reached toward me with it. "Every time you make me break one of these," he began. Then he smiled this evil, sick smile. "Every time, I am going to mark you with it. So you remember that you are *not* better than me. I am superior! You are inferior. I am handsome, you are ugly! We'll see how long it takes you to learn your lesson. How smart is Jen? Oh, she thinks she's *so* smart, but she's really, really stupid!" He had begun to circle me again while he spoke. He would slide the edge of the glass on me in random places, my side, my thigh, arm, breast. Then he was in front of me again and stopped once more. "Stupid people need help remembering. Since I love you, I'm going to help you remember. Lay on the floor!" he said. I lay down on my back. He knelt over me, straddling me, pinning my arms to my sides with his knees. He touched the bruise that was forming on my ribs from the kick earlier. He frowned and looked in my eyes. "That needs a partner, something to match it." The bruise was on my right side. He took the broken glass and wrote "Stupid" on my left side. He pressed harder in some places than other. Here and there, the glass cut through my skin and drew blood. I felt it trickling down in a few places. He looked at it critically, then swiped his hand across, smearing the blood. "It's not right! It didn't turn out right!" he yelled. He stood up, set the glass on a shelf, and flipped me over. He pulled me up on the bed, face down with my legs hanging over. Then he raped me from behind. He pushed my face into the mattress so I could barely breathe. The whole time he was raping me, he was muttering and groaning, "It's not right. You have *no* right to make *me* feel *bad*! It's not *right*! I'm in control! I *own* you!" 21

I tried to push my head up to breathe and he punched me in the back. I turned my head to the side. He wrapped his hand in my hair. "No one said you could move!" he sneered. "You are *done* having fun during love making! I'm in control. I decide." But he had lost his erection and couldn't finish. "We'll continue this later," he said. "You can finish unpacking now." Then he stood up and left the room. I heard the TV being turned up and a beer opening. I sat up and looked at my side. "Stupid" in an angry red welt with a few bloody places was visible, but probably wouldn't scar. At least not my skin, but I felt the weight of that word drumming into my brain. How stupid I had been to think I could outmaneuver John. I realized the next three months weren't going to be as easy as I had thought.

I dressed and went to put the kitchen together. First I had to clean up the Kool-Aid mess and broken glass. Mechanically, I put dishes, pots, and pans away in the cupboards. I didn't pay much attention to where I was putting things. When the kitchen was done, I set up the bathroom and took a shower. I felt I had let myself down and couldn't face my reflection in the mirror.

"Get out here!" John barked. He was on the couch closest to the TV with two beers. Both were opened. He made a show of choosing one and handed it to me. He grinned and wiggled his eyebrows at me in what I'm sure he thought was a seductive look, but really was comical. I didn't laugh. "Drink up!" he said. "We're celebrating our first night in our new home, our very own place, where no one can bother us or interrupt us ever again!" I knew my beer was drugged. I drank it anyway. 13, 18, 23

The next day, I knew John had finished what he had started in raping me. I couldn't remember anything past sitting with him on the couch, watching a movie, and drinking one beer after another. But I knew he had used me. Looking in the bathroom mirror, I could see a bite mark on my back that was new. I really hurt between my legs, but I needed to hurry or I would be late for work. He was cheerful and acted like it was the best day ever. He dropped me off, promising to be there right on time at 12:30 a.m. "But we might have to stay late," I told him. We had to stay until the work for the night was done. "Just call me and let me know," he crooned and gave me a big sloppy kiss. He was all goofy from the half dozen pills he'd already taken to chase away his hangover.

I was quiet that night at work. Not many people were on the night shift. There were about eight of us "keyers" doing data entry and about six "arbors" or property locators, in the room next to ours. The few guys in computer processing were in the next building. We only saw them at the end of the shift to hand over the work. The janitor and his wife didn't clean on Sunday nights. I got some teasing from the ladies I worked with about celebrating too much the night before. They knew we had moved in Saturday and assumed I was hung over. I guess I was. I don't really know how much I drank. I let them make their assumptions and kept quiet. I was going to have to conserve my energy to survive. I began to make my own assumptions. I thought if I stayed alert and stood up to John, I would have a fighting chance. I drank more coffee at work than usual. I decided I wasn't going to just roll over and play dead. I called and let John know when to pick me up. He was in really good spirits. He had a drink for me in the car. I "accidentally" spilled it. I didn't want to be drugged again, especially not two nights in a row. He got mad and threw the glass across the car. Of course, it broke.

When we got to the apartment, he stayed behind in the car. I went ahead and let myself in. It was the last time I ever did that. He came in a minute later with some shards of glass in his hand. "Give me your key!" he demanded. "Why?" I asked. "I need it," he said. "Did you lose yours already?" I asked. I couldn't believe it! He was so incompetent! I started to ask where he last remembered having it, but he cut me off. He got right in my face and shouted, "Give me your key! You will not leave me alone like that again! Everyone saw me having to clean up *your* mess!" At first, I didn't know what he was talking about. It was 1:00 a.m. No one, but us was even awake, I was sure of it. "Let's just look for your key," I replied. I was shaking inside, but tried to remain calm. "Was it on your key ring?" He grabbed hold of me and shoved me onto the nearest couch. He wrapped his left hand in my hair and held the glass shards to my breast. "I didn't lose *my* key!" he sneered. "I'm confiscating yours. You need to be kept in line!" He jabbed the glass into my breast, then got up, and stalked over to my purse, taking some of my hair with him. He found our apartment key on the ring and took it off. He slipped it into his pocket and turned back to me, all smug. "From now on, you leave when I *let* you leave, got it?" he challenged. I tried to think of a way out, but my mind was frozen. I didn't want to be locked in this place with no way out. The deadbolt was one that had to be opened with a key on the inside as well as the outside. 23

Finally, I thought of something. "What if I have to go to the laundry room and you aren't here?" I asked. He snorted and rolled his eyes, advancing on me. He leaned over me as I cowered on the couch, trying not to show fear and failing. "You can't even *iron!*" he yelled. "I'm not letting you *touch* my clothes to try and launder them. Who knows what color they'll turn out to be or how badly you will shrink them!" He was so close to me, our noses almost touched. I could feel his spit spraying my face. "I've done laundry before!" I said. "I'm not an idiot!" That set him off. All I remember is his eyes boring into me like big black holes. His hands grabbed my wrists and he dragged me down the hall. I woke up the next morning. That's it. The whole night is black—no memory whatsoever. I wasn't drunk or drugged, but I could not remember anything. I was on the edge of the bed closest to the wall. It was the side John designated as mine. I opened my eyes. John was staring at me. I started to get up and that's when the pain hit; everything inside and out, hurt terribly. I winced and fell back on the bed. "You really weren't very good last night," John said. Then he shoved me out of bed with his feet and left the room. I stayed on the floor until he finished showering and was eating breakfast.

Gingerly, I made my way to the bathroom. As I carefully washed, I realized I was covered in bruises, bite marks, foot prints from being kicked. Dried blood clung to my left breast and made a trail where he had stuck me with the glass shards last night. I have no memory of them being pulled out. After dressing, I went to the kitchen to get a bowl of cereal for breakfast. "Oh no," he said. "Bad girls don't get any breakfast. Besides, I noticed you seem to have put on some weight lately." I knew I hadn't. I weighed myself every weekend at home. I weighed ninety-five pounds, just like I had for the last two years. I told him as much and he punched me in the stomach. Instantly, I doubled over. "You want to argue with me?" he yelled. "I know what I see! You are getting fat! Too bad, it's not with my baby! Then at least you'd be good for *something!*" He felt very slighted and angry that he couldn't get me pregnant. I was glad. The last thing I needed was a lifelong tie to him! He blamed me though. He said I "wasn't woman enough to get pregnant."

He stood over me in the kitchen, yelling that even a *dog* can get knocked up, but not me. I was still doubled over, trying not to get sick. John decided I wasn't really listening to him and what he had to say was *important!* I was being disrespectful to him, as usual. He grabbed my arm and pulled me into the bathroom. He shoved me against the sink and pushed my face in the mirror. "Look!" he demanded. "Look at your ugly self!" He pulled on my hair until I opened my eyes. As I stared at him in the mirror, seeing him glaring at me, I hated him! He was like a wild man, yet also very much in control. "Repeat after me," he demanded "I'm Jennifer." I kept silent. He knew I didn't like my formal name. I usually went by Jenny. He and his family had called me Jen from the beginning. His grip tightened on my hair. I felt several strands popping out. My head was the least hurt part of me at that time. He hadn't hit me in the face since that first time when he'd split my lip open. His eyes met mine in the mirror. "Repeat!" he gritted out. "Or I'll make you wish you were dead!"

"I already do!" I spat back.

Then he grinned, his sick, ugly, smug grin and said, "No, you don't. Not yet, but you will. You have no idea the things I have planned for you!" He was so calm, it was eerie.

Then he suddenly let go of my hair, spun me, and slammed me into the wall by the sink. He grabbed my hair on both sides of my head and slammed my head back, hard. "Repeat!" he demanded again. My head was spinning. I felt sick and was seeing stars. Then slam, again. "Repeat!" Finally, with tears streaming down my face, I obeyed and repeated, "I'm Jennifer." He leaned in close and whispered in my ear, "See that wasn't so hard. Why do you have to make everything so hard on me?" Then he had me repeat what became a never-ending, never-changing mantra that we went through on an almost daily basis. He called it "the lessons." The only change was where they were held—sometimes facing the bathroom mirror, sometimes in the other rooms with my purse mirror or no mirror at all. But always these words: I'm Jennifer, I'm ugly, I'm fat, I'm stupid, I'm worthless, I'm useless, I talk too much, no one loves me but John, no one will ever love me like John does.

Once, I whispered "Thank God" at the end. I don't know what happened after I did. Everything went black. I was not allowed to deviate in any way from repeating him exactly. I had to keep my eyes open, looking either at him or at my reflection and speak up or he started all over again. He would sigh and lament that he had to be *so* patient with me. I was so stupid and forgetful. He was sure no one else in the world would have his patience.

I tried standing my ground for about a week. He hadn't been so violent before we moved in. Even then, it had been only an occasional outburst. But now, he woke up each day with an agenda. I realized he had a plan—a well-thought-out plan—and I had played right into it! My family did not know where I was. He had forbid me from telling them. He took the phone with him every time he left. He literally unplugged it from the wall, tucked it in his jacket, and walked out, locking the dead bolt behind him. 3, 23

He came home early from work on Monday that first week announcing that he had hurt his back lifting a patient. He was on workmen's compensation until his back healed. So now my only reprieve was when I went to work. After standing my ground didn't work, I tried just being quiet, staying out of his way and not setting him off. But he pursued me relentlessly. Once he had an idea, there was *no* dissuading him.

He had taken me to my parent's house that first week, in the middle of the night. We raided my mom's big, upright freezer. He insisted they owed us meat as a housewarming gift, even though they weren't allowed to know where I was. We took steak, ribs, sausage, hamburger, and chicken. He also brought my bird to our apartment that night. I had made arrangements with my younger sisters to feed Ken for me and clean his cage, but John insisted on bringing him. Ken had been one of John's Christmas gifts to me, besides the engagement ring. He was a pretty green and yellow parakeet. John had named him Ken when I had taken too long choosing a name. He had been disappointed when I didn't bring Ken over on move-in day, and of course, he never let anything go. So Ken was brought into the hell that John was making. I did not have a good feeling about it. Especially since the next day, John gave me a kitten. He named it Tippy. The downstairs neighbor, a single mom with a son about five or six years old, had given it to John. Tippy was an orange-pointed Siamese with blue eyes. I loved him at first sight. It was a big mistake to let John see how much I loved Tippy. 25

John had been busy getting to know the neighbors. Everyone loved him! The apartment manager, Barb, called him "Son" and he called her "Mom." He helped her with chores, like trimming bushes, pulling weeds, cleaning the pool. She thought he was the sweetest, most hardworking, thoughtful young man around. He became friends with some neighbors in the middle wing on the second floor. They had moved in about the same time as us. It was a husband, wife, and a six-year-old girl. The wife had been put on bed rest because of an ectopic pregnancy. John helped them finish unpacking. We went over to their place a few times to party, but soon, John would go without me. That was fine with me. Then I didn't have to keep up appearances that things were normal. "Normal" would not describe what went on in our apartment!

We had the new neighbors over for dinner one night, early on. John dictated the menu. He wanted meatloaf and mashed potatoes. The neighbors brought salad and rolls. It was supposed to be our mutual housewarming party. I couldn't find my potato masher when it came time to use it. I knew I had one. It was part of a set I had. But it was nowhere to be found. The neighbor went and got her mixer and used it to mash the potatoes. John made a great show of how she had saved the day and the dinner, as opposed to my inexperience and incompetence.

I remember showing Tippy and Ken to the little girl and trying to ignore John. Nothing I did or didn't do was right as far as he was concerned. When the neighbors left, John let me know just how humiliated he was by my inability to make mashed potatoes. "They're just potatoes and you mash them! How hard is that? You can't even find the fucking masher! She had to go home and bring back *her* stuff to mash them with. You are pathetic! Disgusting! How could I even want to *be* with you!? You're an idiot!" He was on a roll and I started tuning him out. He finally realized I wasn't listening. If fact, I was thinking he had probably hid the masher to make me look bad.

He came at me in a rage. I thought we were going to go through the "lessons" again, but he dragged me over to the TV. I had put Ken's cage on it. It was just a small wire cage about twelve inches by eighteen inches. It sat on a cardboard box I had cut down and lined with newspaper. As he held my hair in one hand, he flipped the latch and got Ken out with the other. Then he went to the couch where Tippy was sleeping, dragging me with him by my hair. I knew what he was planning. I started begging him, "Please, John, please don't! I'm sorry. I'll be good. I'm so sorry. It won't happen again! Please!" He let go of my hair and sat down next to Tippy. He kicked me and snarled, "Did I give you permission to speak?" This was another of his new lessons he was trying to teach me. Inferior species like me had no right to do *anything* without a superior being like him giving them the idea and then the permission to do it. Everything from using the bathroom, speaking, dressing, etc., was done only when and how he allowed.

I dropped my eyes and waited. "Look at me," he commanded. "Look at what you make me do." I fearfully looked up. John was sitting there fuming with Ken perched on a finger. He was petting Tippy, who was starting to wake up. He moved Ken closer to Tippy. Ken started moving nervously back and forth on John's finger. "So are you going to be good? Are you going to behave?" John asked.

"Yes." I nodded.

"Are you going to *listen* when I speak?" he yelled. By now, Tippy was wide awake and getting interested in Ken. He stood up and started sniffing in Ken's direction. John continued to hold Ken just out of Tippy's reach and stared at me. I pleaded with my eyes since I had not been given permission to speak. Suddenly, John smacked Tippy and stood up. "Bad kitty!" he said, "Just like your owner." He put Ken back in his cage. 19, 20

He came back and stood over me while I snuggled Tippy. "You get it now? Stupid, ugly bitch?" he yelled. "You see what you are going to make me do someday? What you are going to *drive* me to?" I nodded yes, blinking back tears. John reached down and pulled Tippy off my lap. "I don't think you do, stupid, ugly bitch! I don't think you understand anything!"Tippy cried out from the way John was holding him. He must have scratched John because he suddenly flung Tippy into the drapes, cussing and holding his thumb. Tippy was tangled in the drapes. We had gotten in trouble with Barb earlier that day over snags that Tippy had put in the drapes. They were these filmy, light-colored sheers and every little snag showed. Barb said they were new and we'd had to pay $100 for a pet deposit. I got up to extract him, but John shoved me across the room. "No one said you could move!" he raged. "I can see we are going to be up all night with your lessons, stupid, ugly bitch!" He grabbed my feet and dragged me to the bathroom. 15

"Lesson 1: Bad girls don't get to keep dinner. We're going to play a game. It's called 'How many punches does it take to make a stupid, ugly bitch throw up?'" He made me stand up with my back against the sink. He pinched my waist, shaking his head. "Despite my best efforts, you are getting fat." He punched me in the gut, hard. He lifted the toilet seat, smiled, and said, "Ready when you are!" and punched me again. It took five punches before I threw up dinner. 8

Then he made me clean up the kitchen while he watched TV. After that, he got out the leftover mashed potatoes. There were a lot of them. He had peeled over five pounds of potatoes. He had said he wanted to help me with dinner. It always caught me off guard how he switched from one mood to the next in the blink of an eye. How much was calculated and how much was spur of the moment, I never knew. He had been sweet and cheerful, peeling away, while I put together the meatloaf. He had talked about how nice it was to work side by side with his best girl in the kitchen. Now, he was being overly sweet again. Petting my head, saying how surely I must be hungry. He took the cover off the bowl of potatoes and smashed my face in it. "Eat them!" he demanded. "Eat them all!" I had no spoon, but I scooped them up with my fingers and ate while he stood there glaring at me. Then he made me wash the bowl and my face, which still had potato on it. He made me put my face in the running water to scrub off the potato. The sink was still plugged on that side and filled up. He held my head under the water until I sucked some into my lungs. Then he pulled me out, choking and gasping. Just when I started to catch my breath, he plunged me back in. It took three times before I gagged hard enough to vomit the potatoes. "Hmm, interesting," he said. He released his grip on the back of my neck and said, "Clean up this mess and go to bed." He got a beer and went to watch TV.

By the time I was in my pajamas, I could breathe fairly normally. My abdomen and neck were sore and my chest ached. But considering the previous beatings I had endured, I thought I got off lucky. I was wrong. No sooner was I in bed, than he busted through the door. "What the hell do you think you are doing, stupid, ugly bitch?" he screamed, flicking on the light. I forgot myself and croaked out, "You told me to go to bed."

"You're going to talk back to me? You really are the dumbest dog on the planet, bitch! I want a beer. I want you to sit with me and watch this movie. I didn't risk my life getting this HBO unit so you could ignore me! *Get up!*" he yelled. I jumped out of bed. "Get dressed in something sexy. I'm gonna want loving later and I need to be put in the mood," he sneered. I started looking through my dresser. I had no idea what he would think was sexy and I really didn't have much in the way of lingerie. He came up behind me, slapping me upside the head. "Get out of my way, cow!" he said. "I will look. You don't know sexy from a hole in the wall." He dumped all four of my drawers onto the floor. Everything was in a pile: t-shirts, socks, bras, panties, shorts, pjs, swimsuits, and sweats. He picked through the pile, holding up random items, shaking his head and tossing them aside.

Suddenly, he viciously kicked out, getting me in the thigh. I dropped to the floor. He stood over me, breathing heavily. Through clenched teeth, he said, "Didn't I tell you to get dressed?" I nodded. He kicked me again, in the hip. "Well," he spat in my face, "you can't get dressed if you don't take those fucking pajamas off!" I pulled my dorm shirt off over my head. "The panties too" he said. He grabbed a bikini I hadn't worn in two years, sighed, and flung it at me. "I guess this will have to do," he said. I put it on and followed him to the living room. "Get us some beer," he demanded. I got two beers. We sat there drinking and watching some nasty movie. I had no idea how he got this channel, but I knew what he was going to do with me when the movie was over. I downed as many beers as I could. He bought the cheapest beer he could find. It was gross, but it was better than being sober for sex with John. I blacked out the rest of that night. From drinking or just my mind shutting down, I don't know. I do know he had fun because I was really sore again the next morning.

He was in a great mood. He took the dirty laundry down to do it for me, so I could rest, he said. He made coffee and poured me a cup. When I took a drink, he slapped the cup out of my hands. "You drink when I say you drink!" he said. "Now, since you don't appreciate *anything* I do for you, I'm going to help Barb outside." He shook his head at me and said, "Man, that's bad when even a lesbian knows how to treat a man better than *you* do!" (Barb was gay and lived in the apartment on the first floor, closest to the parking lot with her girlfriend.) He slammed and locked the door. I heard him whistling as he walked away. 13, 21

Looking out the window, I watched and listened. He called down to Barb that he had to go to his car for a second. I ran to the bedroom and watched him toss the phone in and cover it with his jacket. Then he went to help his new best girl. That is what he had started calling her. He used to call me his best girl, but now I was stupid, ugly bitch or Jennifer or Jocelyn, my mom's name. He delighted in calling me by my mom's name. I had always thought it was a pretty name until he started saying it. John made it sound like a cuss word. I felt very far from my family. I didn't think I would ever see them again.

I sat drinking coffee, listening to John and Barb joke and tease below. I had opened the little window by the front door and turned off the air conditioner. It wasn't hot enough to even need it. I think John just liked to run it to make me cold. I had frozen the night before in my bikini, watching his stupid porno movie. I remembered that I hadn't put my clothes back in the drawers. When I went to put them away, I found my potato masher. It was just lying on top of the pile of clothes, like it had always been there! I knew it wasn't there last night. John had taken it, just like I thought! He had set me up and then punished me. I put it back in the kitchen drawer and put my clothes away. I felt helpless, but not yet defeated.

John came in later to shower and have lunch. He said he had some errands to run. "Do you need anything?" he asked. I told him to get cigarettes and more beer. Amazingly, for reasons I never figured out, John allowed me unlimited beer and cigarettes. Those were the only things he did not restrict or control. He said he would get them and promised an additional present. He assured me I would be delighted. I thanked him sweetly and he left, whistling merrily. From the outside, it looked like we were just two kids in love, starting out on our own. I'm sure the neighbors had to hear the yelling and my head being repeatedly slammed into the walls and floor, but so far, no one had said a thing about it or come to help.

I looked in the fridge. There was still about a twelve-pack of beer left. It was barely 1:00 p.m., but I started drinking. I decided that this was one thing I could control, at least when John wasn't around to make me drink or drug my drink. It was Saturday, I didn't have to work and I wanted to take the edge off my hangover. I was learning that drinking helped to dull the pain—all different types of it.

By the time John came back a few hours later, I was pleasantly buzzed. He had something in his jacket. I figured it was the phone, so I kept watching TV. "Well, hello to you too!" he said and pulled his white bunny out with a flourish. He dropped her to the floor and stomped over to me. "I said I was bringing you a surprise and you don't even get up to greet me!" he raged. Never mind the fact that I'm not allowed to move or talk without his permission! I just grinned stupidly up at him. It had occurred to me that maybe if I let him think I was drunker than I really was, he would leave me alone. I was wrong.

The next day, I woke up just in time to throw some clothes on and have John drive me to work. I hurt so badly all over. I had noticed some new bruises—dark, ugly blotches on top of the old yellow-green and not so old, bluish ones. But of course, nothing on my face. He was careful about that. I had begun pulling away from the other ladies at work. I couldn't seem to join in with their stories and jokes. I certainly couldn't tell them what was happening and I didn't have it in me to lie. So I mostly kept quiet unless directly asked a question. They would tease and say, "Jenny's so in love, her head is in the clouds!"

It had now been two weeks in the apartment. I was nervous, on edge, and jumpy a lot of the time, especially with John. Work was my only refuge. My friend, Kari, invited me for Chinese food, but I didn't have any money. "We just got paid Thursday," she said. "I know, but I don't have any on me," I explained. I wasn't going to tell her that John always took all my money as soon as I got paid. "Well, I'm buying," she said, "to celebrate your new place." So we went to our favorite place and got take-out. It was so good! I didn't remember eating anything Saturday, just drinking. Most of Friday's food had been thrown up. I left my take-out box in the break room refrigerator for the next few nights. This way I could eat without John's interference. I thought I was being smart. 22

I don't know how he knew. Maybe he spied on us. He knew what time our dinner break was at. I didn't think to watch for him or his car. He seemed distracted when he picked me up, like he had something on his mind. I didn't ask. It wasn't a healthy thing to ask John questions. As soon as we stepped inside, John kicked me hard. I fell and he was on me, pinning me down. "You have something you want to say?" he asked.

"No," I said.

"Really, how stupid do you think I am?" he asked. He was calm, but I could tell he was boiling on the inside. "I don't think you're stupid," I answered.

"That's right," he smiled. "I'm *not* the stupid one. *You* are! You need a new nickname. One I can use in front of company, one that's a secret code—just between us." He seemed to be moving to a new topic. He leaned back, squashing my stomach. He sat there looking thoughtful and then his face lit up. "I've got it!" he cried. "S.U.B.! it's perfect! It stands for, now say it with me: Stupid, Ugly Bitch—which of course, is what *you* are! But no one else will know that, now, will they, S.U.B.? But instead of saying S.U.B., I'll just call you SUB. It'll be our little secret, just between us." 8

He pinched my breast, twisting hard, and leaned into my face. "Now do you want to tell me what you ate at work, or do we have to see it in the toilet to figure it out, SUB?" he snarled. He knew! How? I don't know, but he definitely knew, or maybe he was guessing. Either way, I was caught. Instead of punches, he played, "How many kicks does it take to make SUB throw up?" It took three. As I lay on the cold bathroom floor, clutching my stomach, I thought, *At least I got to keep it down for a few hours. Surely, I digested something in that amount of time.*

When I came out of the bathroom, John had a new game. In each of his hands was a slip of paper with a word written on it. One said "Loving" and one said "Punishment." For me, it meant the same. John never said rape. He never admitted to raping me. It was always "loving," as far as he was concerned. He smiled sweetly and held out his fists. "You get to choose tonight's activity," he said. Then he pulled his fists back a little and said, "Ah, but choose wisely now." I picked a hand. The paper in that hand said, "Loving." "Great!" he exclaimed, jumping up and down. "I was hoping you'd pick that one! I sooo do love making love to you!" he emphasized the word *love* each time.

"Get us some beers. I'll find a movie," he said. When I came back with the beer, there was another porno movie on the TV. He took a beer and patted the couch next to him. When I sat down, he spilled his beer on me. It was on purpose. He just turned and poured it all over me. "That will teach *you* to sit without permission. Go get naked and come back!" he yelled. I left the room. This permission thing tripped me up all the time. John was very consistent with it in the beginning, but he would let a little slip go, now and then. The next slip, he would pounce on and viciously punish me. As time went on, he let more slide, only to suddenly enforce it again. I never knew from one moment to the next how he would react to anything.

John had received some things from Worker's Comp., besides more prescription drugs. They had given him an egg-crate foam pad for the bed and an electric muscle stimulator to wear. The foam pad covered most of the bed. He did not allow me to sleep on it. I ended up with about twelve inches of bed between the foam pad and the edge. That was fine by me. I could stay farther away from John. I didn't fall out of bed, much.

The muscle stimulator was a new thing doctors were trying. It came with a belt that you strapped on. This held the little box against the injury. The box released mild electric pulses that were supposed to stimulate healing. John loved that box. He took it apart as soon as he got back with it. He started messing with the wiring, adding bigger batteries and trying to see how much of a shock he could get out of it. He was obsessed with it and with trying it out on me. I don't think he ever wore it once since his back injury was faked anyway! He didn't need its help to heal, but he was convinced it could be effective in my "training"!

He had taken my plans to be a tutor and turned them against me. From the day we moved in, he said that a tutor needs to know "lots of things" in order to teach them to others. He was going to teach me all these things. That was supposedly the point of the lessons and all his other sick games. I didn't think I needed to know anything he tried to teach me. At first, I had tried to learn and play along, hoping for a pattern to help me navigate this *hell*. But so much of it was random or inconsistent. It was impossible to anticipate or predict his next move.

I left my beer-soaked clothes on the bathroom floor and started looking for something to wear. I had few clean clothes and was really cold. John controlled the laundry as well as the thermostat. He often didn't wash my stuff. I sensed him behind me and turned. I couldn't help it; I covered myself with my hands as best I could. He stood in the doorway and ordered me to turn around with my hands at my sides. I did, and when I was facing him again, he had tears in his eyes. I thought he was moved by all the damage visible on my body. Boy, was I wrong! He came forward and held my face between his hands. "You are looking so much more beautiful now than when we moved in!" he whispered. "I don't need a movie to inspire me. Let's love right now!" He planted a big sloppy kiss on my mouth. It was all I could do not to gag.

It was awful to be the center of his attentions and totally sober on top of it! He was rough and seemed to delight in poking or massaging my most painful spots. It took forever for him to finish. I wished desperately to black out, but did not. When he was finally done, he pushed me onto the floor. "You are on my side of the bed," he stated coldly. Of course, that was where he had made me lie down. I knew better than to argue. "Now you have to be punished! You ruin everything! We just had the best time and you ruin it with your disobedience! I warned you to stay on your *own* side, damn dog! You *never* do what I say, do you?" he yelled. I had just spent hours doing what he said, but obviously, that didn't count. He stomped out and came back with his muscle stimulator. I had no idea how much of a shock it gave. I really did not want to find out. But I did find out, and then, thankfully, I blacked out the rest of that night. 21

I slept really late the next day. John was still sleeping. I dressed, found the key in his pants, and let myself out to go to work. Riding on the bus, aching and throbbing in pain, I wondered how much more I could take. What more could he do to me? I didn't want to think about it. I decided to try hiding. Maybe if he couldn't find me, he'd give up on whatever sick game he was planning and leave me alone. I guess I really was turning stupid. Hiding lasted two days. He always found me and was furious that I had dared to defy him.

We were having his parents over for dinner that Friday. He said we were terribly off schedule for their visit because of my hiding. According to John, it had fucked everything up. I made the mistake of asking, "What schedule?"

"Your training schedule, fucking SUB!" he raged. "Do you think you are *anywhere* near ready to have my parents here? You disobey me at every turn. *And in my own house,* fucking SUB! My own house!" He was nearly bawling like a baby. Since I was paying the bills, I didn't really think of it as John's own house, but obviously, he did. He was still ranting about being humiliated in front of his dad with my bad behavior. How it would look bad that he had no control of his woman, his household. I promised I would be on my best behavior and he actually started crying. "That's exactly what I'm talking about!" he whined.

"What?" I asked.

He stormed up to me and shouted in my face, "You don't even have *my* permission to speak right now! Damn! Dog, you can't get the simplest, tiniest thing right! We have been working on this for weeks! And still you are *so stupid!* I can't believe how stupid you are! I'm beginning to think you are hopeless, a lost cause." 8, 25

Then I made a big mistake. I told him he could just give up on me, let me go home, and forget he ever knew me. Instantly, his tears dried up. He wound his hands up in my hair on each side of my face. I knew what was coming. He backed me into the wall. Slowly and menacingly, he snarled in my face, "You'd like that, wouldn't you? You'd like to go home to your nice boring room and your nice boring dad and your stupid, uptight, frigid mom and your dumb little sisters and your fucking shithead brother, Marky!" He was yelling now. Then the head slamming began. With each word he spoke, he slammed my head into the wall behind me. "You don't get off that easy! I'm still having fun with you!" He tried to fling me aside, but his hands were still wrapped in my hair, so I didn't go far. He started kicking me over and over, yelling, "Get away from me, whore! Stupid, ugly bitch! I don't want to see your fucking ugly face right now!" He pulled his hands away, taking hair with them. As I lay there, gasping, my head spinning, I wondered how I even had any hair left.

John told his parents I couldn't cook, so they had to bring the main dish and dessert. He said he would make the sides. He told his mom to make corned beef and cabbage with German chocolate cake. He knew I hated both of those. Just the smell of corned beef and cabbage made me nauseated.

Friday came too quickly. As I cleaned that day, I realized how messed up the apartment was getting. John had spilled countless glasses of Kool-Aid on the carpet. Nothing I used got the stains out. The drapes were snagged more than ever. He had glued coins to the refrigerator with super glue, for some unknown reason. His rabbit had free rein of the place. He insisted she used Tippy's litter box, but I never found any rabbit droppings in it when I cleaned it. I did find rabbit droppings everywhere else. I showed him a pile of them I found in a corner by the TV. He accused me of taking them out of the litter box and putting them there! It was absurd! I denied it, but he insisted I had. He told me to pick them up. I started to go get a paper towel, but he stopped me. "Where the hell do you think you are going? I said to pick them up!" he screamed. So I gathered them in my hands. At least they were dry and not fresh. "Now eat them!" he demanded.

"No!" I gasped.

"Do we really have to go over the lessons again today?" he asked. "If you don't eat them, I will let Tippy eat Ken."

"John, please be reasonable. They're droppings!" I was getting frantic.

"I am being reasonable. We both know you won't be eating what's for dinner, so you have to eat something. I'm only looking out for you, and as usual, I get *no* appreciation for it!" He turned around and started calling Tippy. Tippy had no fondness for John. He had been hurt by him and didn't trust him anymore. But John found him sleeping on the floor by my side of the bed. He brought Tippy in the living room. "Are you going to eat your dinner, or is Tippy having a Ken sandwich?" he asked. He seemed so calm, like he was asking if I wanted fries with my burger. I hesitated. He had made this particular threat more than once. Always trying to get me to do something I didn't want to, go one step further, sink a little lower. But he'd never followed through because I always caved and did what he wanted. Would he really do it? He opened Ken's cage and reached for him. Ken started flapping around in the cage. Tippy was squirming and mewing. I was stuck. I didn't want Ken or Tippy to get hurt. I didn't know if John really would go through with it. But God, I didn't want to eat this bunny poo! John had Ken in his hand now, pulling him out of the cage. He set Ken down on the floor and crouched next to him with Tippy. He had done this before, threatening to let go of Tippy so he could pounce on Ken, but this time, Ken flew away. I hadn't trimmed his wings since before we moved in. *Go, Ken, go!* I thought. 19

"Shit!" John exclaimed and took off down the hall after Ken. I ran into the kitchen and hid the droppings in the trash. Then I picked up Tippy and sat back on the couch. Just then there was a knock on the door. It was way too early for his parents, but whoever it was, I couldn't open the door. It was locked like always. "John," I called, "someone is at the door!" He stomped up to me, grabbed Tippy, and threw him across the room. "Put that bird back and finish cleaning!" he hissed at me. I took off for the bedroom and he got the door. It was Barb. She asked John to move his car. It was parked in someone else's spot. He said he would move it right away and shut the door. I had captured Ken and was putting him away. John came up behind me and said, "We will postpone our lessons until after the dinner party. I have lots in store for you, SUB!" As I straightened up, I realized that the only clean clothes I had would show my bruises and other marks. When John got back from moving his car, I asked if I could do some laundry. "You!" he snorted. "Do laundry? You can't even make fucking mashed potatoes! No way can you operate a washer and dryer."

"Well, I need some clothes washed. I have nothing to wear." I explained.

He mimicked me, "I have nothing to wear. Oh, boo-hoo! Oh, woe is me! What do you think you should wear, SUB?" This was a trap. I knew it. Yet I had to answer or suffer the consequences. 8, 23

"I should wear something pretty," I said. "Something that makes you proud to be seen with me." He slapped himself gently upside his head, looking astonished. "Well, she can be taught after all!" he exclaimed. "So go pick out something pretty, my pretty, little SUB. Go on now, I give you permission." He smiled encouragingly at me. Was he really this ignorant or just toying with me? I couldn't tell. "Everything I have, that's clean, is like what I'm wearing now," I said carefully. He stared at me with his huge glassy black eyes. I held out my arms, lifted one leg, showing him the multicolored skin visible past my t-shirt sleeves and shorts. My heart was pounding. The littlest thing could set him off without warning. Finally, he asked, "What have you been wearing?"

"Long sleeves and pants," I replied. It was surreal. This was the longest, most normal conversation we'd had in three weeks.

Suddenly, he jumped up in the air, all lanky and gangly. "Well, I best be getting some laundry done for my SUB then, huh?" he said and winked at me. I handed him the basket of clothes and he left for the laundry room. Now I was really on edge. Usually, he was the most vicious immediately after he was the sweetest. If you can call anything he did being sweet, since there was always an ulterior motive behind it.

I cleaned the bathroom and made the bed, shaking the whole time. I dreaded him coming back. Then the phone rang. My heart jumped to my throat. At first, I didn't know what it was. I couldn't believe he had left the phone! I didn't know what to do. Answer it, ignore it. Who could it even be? I decided to answer it. The bill was in my name, so that made it my phone as far as I was concerned. John couldn't get any of the utilities in his name because of the Trans-Am repossession. It was John. He said, "Hi! How's my SUB getting along without me?" I could tell he was really high. He said he was hanging out with Barb and her girl until the laundry was done. I hung up, relieved. At least I had some time to myself. I decided to take a nice relaxing shower alone. Usually, if John was awake when I showered, he sat on the toilet watching me and pointing out every flaw he could think of. This would be nice for a change. Maybe it would help calm my nerves.

I had just finished rinsing out the shampoo and putting conditioner on my hair when the shower curtain flew open. I spun around. John was getting in the tub, naked and semi-erect. "Starting without me, I see," he said. I knew better than to say a word. He soaped me up, rough as always. He was muttering under his breath how I had been a bad girl. Bad girls needed a thorough cleaning to make them presentable. He held me under the water to rinse and leaned over, turning off the cold. I couldn't help it. I screamed as the burning hot water hit all my burns and open cuts. I screamed and danced around, trying to get away from the hot spray. He was holding me by my hair with one hand and digging his other into my crotch. "Shut up, whore!" he hissed. "Hold still and take your punishment, SUB." Finally, he turned the cold back on and the temperature evened out. I was gasping and choking. My face had been directly in the stream and I had breathed in some water. "Now that you're clean, let's have some fun before the old farts get here!" he chuckled. Then he proceeded to rape me. He would make me soap him up when he lost his erection and rape me again. Finally, he started shoving things in me: the soap, shampoo bottles, the washcloth. I kept silent as long as I could. When I saw the blood running down the drain, I begged him to stop. My insides hurt so much! He saw the bloody washcloth and chucked it at me in disgust. The only time he left me alone was when I had my period. I hadn't had it yet since we had moved in and I was sure that it hadn't started now, but I wasn't going to share that tidbit of information with John. "You're sick!" he raged. "You know I can't do it when you're on the rag! Why'd you let me? Why didn't you say something?"

He ripped the shower curtain aside and shoved me out. I fell hard on my right side. He pulled the curtain shut, only to open it a second later and pelt me with everything within his reach. "You *bitch!*" he screeched. "You took all the hot water!" He stepped out, wrapped himself in towels, and stomped off to the bedroom. I lay there, stunned. I couldn't stop trembling. This had *not* just happened, had it? Later, he dropped his towels on me and said I better get the mess cleaned up and get myself ready. The "old farts," as he called them behind their backs, would be here soon. "And I want the whole show," he said. "Hair curled, makeup, the works. You owe me after letting me love you when you're at your filthiest!" I heard him open the refrigerator and pop open two beers. He set one on the bathroom counter. "Maybe that will motivate your bloody, lazy ass. *Get up!*" he screamed.

Slowly, trembling like a leaf in the wind, I pushed myself to a sitting position. I shoved the door closed. I needed privacy. I had never felt so violated in my life! All the rapes before had been nothing compared to this one. It took me awhile to get up. I sat on the toilet lid and dried off. I sipped my beer, found some Tylenol, and took four with a swig of beer. I didn't know if it was good or bad, but I was getting used to the taste of this cheap beer. With a towel tight around me, I headed to the bedroom. John had laid out a turtleneck sweater and my favorite pair of jeans. I put on a bra, socks, and panties, then the clothes. My skin felt on fire in places. I was raw and aching between my legs, though not really bleeding much anymore. After combing and blow drying what was left of my hair, I cleaned up the bathroom. I threw the washcloth away. I knew John would never put it in the washer anyway. For spite, I threw away his shampoo too. I didn't even wipe the blood off the bottle. He wouldn't get it out of the trash with blood on it. It was a small but meaningful victory for me. I plugged in the curling iron and started putting on makeup. By the time his parents came, I was all ready and had passed inspection.

That night was pure torture on so many levels. The smell of corned beef and cabbage made me feel sick, just like John knew it would. I could barely sit, I hurt so much. His parent's hugs almost made me cry from the pain they caused. I had to smile and hold hands with this psycho monster like he was the greatest thing in the world. It was unbearable! Having him touch me made my skin crawl. But I had to be nice, charming, and sweet, or I would pay dearly later. I paid anyway.

Nothing I had done or said pleased him. He picked apart everything. "You didn't eat her food!" he pointed out. He knew I wasn't going to when he chose the menu! "You drank too much!" he accused. *Yeah, well, who wouldn't, being around you, Psycho!* I thought to myself. More and more lately, I had stayed silent during his rants. I barely answered him, except to try and avoid a beating. Not that it did much good in that area. On and on he went about one thing after another. I had to pee very badly. I had been holding it as long as I could because it really burned when I went. Finally, I got up and he jumped on me. We both fell to the floor. He had been drinking as much, if not more than me. He straddled me, holding my wrists above my head with one hand. "Where the *fuck* do you think you're going, SUB?" he screamed. "I'm talking to you. Trying to help you better yourself!'

"Please, John!" I begged. "Let me up. I have to pee." He got this evil knowing look on his face. "I haven't given you *permission* to talk, move, or pee!" he yelled. "But since I'm such a nice guy, I've decided to help you—even though you disobey me at every turn." He sat back on top of me, relaxing and letting his full weight rest right on my bladder. He grinned, then began to bounce. "How's that feel?" he asked. I tried to hold it, but I couldn't. I peed my pants right there on the floor. It burned and stung. Tears filled my eyes. He laughed and stood up. As I jumped up to run for the bathroom, he caught my arm. "Clean the carpet first, *dog!*" he sneered. I got some rags and soaked up all the pee I could. In the bathroom, I stripped off my jeans and panties while he stood blocking the doorway. His eyes widened when he saw my panties. "Who said you could wear these?" he stormed.

"I always wear underwear." I replied. "You know that." He backed me up until I hit the tub and fell into it. He leaned over and said, "You wear what I lay out for you to wear! And nothing else! No unauthorized clothes! *Got it? Stupid, ugly bitch!*" I nodded yes. He stormed out cussing and telling me all the infractions I had to be punished for. I rinsed out my jeans and panties and wrung them out as best I could. Then I hung them on the tub to dry. I had no choice, but to leave the bathroom half naked. 8, 18

He was waiting for me in the hall, holding a belt in his hands. He folded it in half, looking solemn, almost sorrowful. Without a word, he followed me into the bedroom. I headed to my dresser, but he stopped me. "Strip," he demanded. I did. "Lay down!" he snapped. I headed to the bed, but he stuck a foot out to trip me. "I said, lay down!" he repeated. "Not, go to bed. We have a lot of work to do, so we need to get started." I hadn't had nearly enough to drink to get through whatever he had in store for me. "God," I prayed silently, "help me, please!" I lay down gingerly. I was actually thankful that he had gone easy on the beatings for a couple of days this week. I had choked down some Chinese food each night at work. I ate as soon as I got there instead of waiting for dinner break. I'm sure he suspected. He had tried to make me throw up a couple of times, but what I had eaten had been digested already. By now, it was shockingly easy for him to make me vomit. Sometimes, I gagged while eating and had to stop. Or a little while after eating, the food would try to come back up. There had still been the lessons every night. He tried to surprise me with the muscle stimulator and played a dozen other mind games. There was always that. But he had let me drink into a stupor two nights and not done anything to me while I was out. At least, not that I could tell.

So there I was, lying flat on my back, praying to get through the next few hours. John started snapping the belt together so it made a loud crack. He smiled this tiny smile each time. "Put your hands under your butt," he ordered. I obeyed and waited. Slowly, he circled me, cracking the belt with a huge grin on his face. "I assume your bladder is empty now," he said, sarcastically. I nodded yes. He sat on me, facing my feet, pinning my hands under me. "Now we have to deal with your clothing disobedience," he stated and grabbed my ankles in his left hand. He slapped my feet repeatedly with that belt. It stung, but I kept quiet. Then I thought, *This is nuts! If I scream enough, someone will surely come or call the cops.* I screamed and he kept at my feet until they were covered in blisters. Finally, he stood up and told me to roll over. I tried to keep my feet off the floor, but he shoved them into the carpet. It was so painful! He sighed and said, "Tuck your hands." I slipped them under me, gripping my upper thighs, clenching my teeth. I was bracing myself for the next attack. He cracked the belt and I jumped. That made him chuckle. "Your fat ass jiggles when you do that!" he said. He cracked it a few more times, then whipped out and struck my backside. I screamed and moved away. He repositioned me. Then he pressed a foot into my back to keep me in place. He went to town on my bottom with that belt. It seemed he would never stop. It drew blood in places and didn't always find its mark, hitting me on the back of the legs. I screamed until my throat was raw. He rolled me over, tucked my hands under me, stepped on me with one foot, and started on my breasts. I blacked out.

I don't know how long I was out. Not too long; it was still night outside, still *hell* inside. He was sitting next to me with a plate of food. "Wow," he said, "punishment sure makes me hungry! How 'bout you? Want some?" he asked and held the plate closer. It was leftovers from that night. I retched and gagged. What beer was left in my stomach came up. He frowned. "Now you've made another mess. I just can't keep up with all your screw-ups, SUB!" he complained with his mouth full of food. I had rolled to my side. My head was swimming, the blisters hurt worse than anything he had done so far. He grabbed my arm, rolled me back, and breathed corned beef and cabbage into my face. I gagged again. Nothing came up this time. "Okay, all done with that show," he announced. He jumped up and left the room. I heard him dump his plate in the sink, open a beer, and then, he was back. He took something off one of the shelves.

He squatted in front of me and held it up. It was a baggie with what looked like dark brown pills in it. Before I could wonder what they would do to me, he began speaking again. "You know I love you, right?" he asked. I didn't respond, but he acted like he didn't notice. "I'm a little concerned, frankly. I mean, we both know you're fat, but still you need to eat *something*. You didn't eat the dinner I offered before the old farts got here and you hardly ate anything while they were here. Honestly, if I didn't know better, I would think you are trying to make me look bad—*again!*" This whole monologue had been spoken quietly, with such calm, but the last word was filled with rage. The baggie was shaking in his hand right in front of my eyes. Just as I realized what was in it, he opened it. "Open your mouth!" he commanded. I actually did open it: to protest. Then he leaned into me holding my mouth open and poured fresh bunny droppings into my mouth before I could react. He put one hand on my mouth, holding it closed, and used his weight to pin me. "Eat!" he yelled. "I can't have people saying I don't take care of my SUB. Now eat! All of them!" I can only assume

I did eat them. I don't know for sure because everything went black. 21

I slept pretty late on Saturday. I was in and out for quite a while. If I could sleep deep enough, I didn't feel too much pain. But eventually, I woke up. It was almost 1:30 p.m. I was on the floor between my side of the bed and the wall. The apartment was quiet. I knew moving was going to be excruciating, but I really had to pee. It took some time to get to the bathroom. I peed and dressed in my dorm shirt. It was long and loose, but still my skin screamed. The apartment was freezing. I couldn't bear socks on my feet. I checked the thermostat. John had set it on 62! I moved it to 75 and went looking for coffee. I found a pot three-fourths full, poured a cup, added milk, and began sipping it.

I was standing in the bedroom with my coffee, looking out the window when John burst in the front door. He was all keyed up, jumping around, waving his arms, and talking excitedly. "Look what I found, SUB!" he squealed. "This is it! This will make the muscle stimulator just right! I can't wait to try it." He skipped back to the dining area and began tinkering with the stuff he kept there. He didn't seem to notice that I didn't respond at all. I was wondering if I would fit through the little window that slid open. I knew I had lost weight, but how much? My clothes hung on me. But that window was pretty small. Slowly, I finished the coffee, along with four more Tylenol, while John worked on his project. I noticed my jeans and panties weren't hanging on the tub. I looked in the hamper, but they weren't there either. I thought about asking John where they were, but I really didn't want his attention directed toward me. I fed the animals, scooped the litter box, thought about a shower, and decided against it. Even with the Tylenol, it would be too painful. Suddenly, John gasped and jumped up. "I forgot all about it in my excitement over the battery!" he exclaimed. "I have another surprise in the car! Help me get it up the stairs." He headed toward the door and unlocked it. I didn't move, but my heart started racing. He had never stopped stealing stuff. His dresser drawers had more stolen electronics in them than clothes: car stereos, CBs, tape decks. He had stolen a bike for the boy who gave us Tippy. He spray painted it out front and Barb got ticked off. He got red paint all over her black wrought-iron railing. He sprayed it black and was back in her good graces again. John was obsessed with this gas BBQ grill he had seen when stealing an HBO unit a couple of months ago. He kept trying to get me to help him steal it. He said it was too heavy for him to take by himself. He'd said if I really loved him, I would want him to be happy and would help him. I wanted nothing to do with it.

Now I was terrified that this was what was in his car. No way was I going to touch it. John had turned and was looking at me. I still hadn't moved. "Never mind," he waved me off. "I'll have the neighbor help me. You're going to love this!" He jumped up and down like a Jack-in-the-box and ran out, slamming the door behind him. I stayed rooted to that spot, numb inside. A little later, I could hear John and the neighbor coming down the walkway. "Open the door, SUB!" he called out. Of course, he hadn't locked it. People couldn't *know* I was locked in all the time. How would that look? I couldn't run out.

The walkway was blocked by John, the neighbor, and whatever it was they were struggling to carry. I opened the door and stepped back. In came John, the neighbor, and the ugliest chair I had ever seen. John was grinning from ear to ear. "Thanks, man," he told the neighbor, who left quickly. "Isn't it great?" he cried out. "I found it! It was just sitting there on the side of the road, waiting for me to pick it up!" It was an ugly green, with rips here and there, stuffing coming out and cobwebs underneath it. "You can have first dibs on it," he offered. I just shook my head no. I started leaving the living room when I heard him say, "I didn't tell you to go anywhere." His voice was cold. Back to business as usual, I thought and began to steel myself for what was coming. 3

He came up behind me, breathing heavily. Calmly, he said, "I got that chair for you. It's a token of my *love!* You are going to sit in it and you are going to *like* it!" No way was I planning on touching that nasty thing! Who knew what might be living in it? For the next hour, we went round and round about the chair. For some reason, he didn't try to physically force me into it. He argued, wheedled, cajoled, and tried to reason with me. It seemed he was determined to "talk" me into sitting in it. Like somehow that would be a victory for him, to have me give in and just do what he said.

Then all of a sudden, he left me alone about the chair and went back to messing with the stimulator. He had a huge battery with coils on top. This was hooked to the stimulator. He continued to mess with it when it must have shocked him good. I heard a buzz and he jumped away, shaking his hand. "Perfect!" he declared. "Now it's ready. SUB, come here!" I had been lying on the couch, listening to the TV. I didn't move. Moving hurt. I wanted to conserve energy for tonight. Since I didn't come to him, he came to me. "Let me show you how good this works now," he said. "It's way better than before." I scrambled off the couch, but I was stiff and slow. As I tried to get past him, he pushed me and I landed in the chair. The filthy, nasty chair! He laughed and laughed. I couldn't get out of it fast enough. My bottom was on fire from the blisters. He followed me, trying to talk me into letting him zap me with the stimulator. He had used it on me before with smaller batteries. I hadn't like it one bit. I went past the dining area into the kitchen, then back through the living room.

I kept going around, trying to keep away from him. "John, please!" I begged. "Leave me alone. I hurt. I just want to lie down!"

"So do it!" he exclaimed. "I will heal you with my new super-duper stimulator!"

"You are *not* touching me with that!" I yelled. "I saw it hurt you!"

"Naw," he answered. "It just surprised me, is all." We were still circling through the apartment. I knew better than to head down the hall. He would trap me in the bedroom. Moving this much was extremely uncomfortable. I was getting mad and told him so. He laughed hard at that and started mocking me. "Oh, SUB's getting *mad!*" he grinned. "Ooooh, I'm so scared! Go ahead, get mad. I can handle it. Let me see what you got!" he egged me on. John had never seen me lose my temper. I had argued with him and yelled during fights. But I had never really lost my temper. I have a very bad temper. It takes a lot for me to lose it, but once I do, it's volatile. I have no control at all over it. He continued to push it with me. I warned him again to leave me alone. We were going through the kitchen and he got close enough to jam the stimulator into my left arm. I was never one of those kids who liked to stick my tongue on a battery. I remember my sisters doing it years ago. I tried it, but it wasn't for me. 1

Electric shock went up my arm all the way to my shoulder. My fingers and lower arm went numb. I saw *red* and I lost it! Spinning toward the cupboards, I screamed, "Now you're going to *die!*" I pulled open the silverware drawer, grabbed the first thing I saw, a large butcher knife, and spun on John. His laugh died away. He backed up, jumping out of the way, as I brought the knife down. Now I was chasing him, furiously looking to kill. He was trying to calm me, promising to leave me alone. But it was too late to calm down. We went around a couple of times with me hot on his trail, but he had more stamina than I did, probably from eating every day. He pulled ahead enough to dart into the bathroom and lock the door. I could hear him ripping the shower curtain as he climbed into the tub. "You think that door is going to save you, asshole?" I shouted. I started chopping the door down with my knife. I didn't get very far before I was winded and out of energy.

It was quiet, eerily quiet, for what seemed a long time. Finally, the buzz in my ears stopped and I could hear the TV in the background. I was lying on the floor, surrounded by little chips of wood from the door. The knife was loose in my hand. Cautiously, John unlocked the door and stepped over me. He took the knife, saying, "That's enough of that." The rest of that day is black. I didn't go to work the next day. I just couldn't move without hurting too much.

By Monday, I could move around a little better. My fingers had sore, swollen joints on some of them. As I examined them, I realized my engagement ring was gone. John had insisted I wear it when we got back together. He saw me looking at my hands, massaging the joints. "I guess you should learn not to try blocking the karate master's kicks," he sneered and walked away. I didn't bother asking where my ring was. I didn't want it anyway. Most of my jewelry had disappeared. I figured he was hocking it to pay for his drugs. No way was his workers comp and my salary paying for everything. I had some silver rings with coral and turquoise that were missing. They had been given to me in high school by a friend. Also a large diamond ring that a guy I dated gave to me. He had even asked me to marry him, but of course, the tenth day came along and ruined that relationship! I knew it was a real diamond because I had cut his name in the corner of the mirror in the girl's PE locker room. Plus I had a few necklaces, bracelets, and lots of earrings. They weren't expensive, but still, they had belonged to me. Now it was all gone, cashed in to fuel his rage that drove him to beat me.

I had begun to lose sight of why I was there in that apartment. My family seemed so far away. Like the distant memory of a movie I had once seen. I had trouble remembering what day it was. I had so many thoughts zip through my head before I could grasp any of them. I wondered if I was losing my mind.

John took me to work. It was hard to do data entry with my hurt fingers. My supervisor commented on how slow I was and that I was making mistakes. I apologized, saying I still wasn't feeling well. During dinner break, Mom called. She wanted to take me out for lunch one day that week for my birthday. I had forgotten my birthday was coming up. I said I would talk to John about it and asked her to call me tomorrow at the same time. She didn't even know we had a phone at the apartment. Now I would have to talk to John. I had been looking forward to ignoring him as much as possible. I had no idea if he would let me go or would insist on joining us. Mom made it clear she wanted me to come alone. The rest of my shift was a blur. If there was a batch of work not signed out, it was me who had taken it and forgotten to initial it. I felt on the verge of tears constantly, but didn't want to break down and have to explain. This was definitely harder than I had bargained for.

When John picked me up, I asked if I could have lunch with my mom for my birthday. He asked where she was taking me. "For Chinese food, since it's my favorite," I replied. "Sure you can, SUB dear. It's not your nineteenth birthday every day, you know," he answered cheerfully. As we were going up the stairs to our apartment, he started going on about how he had cooked dinner for us. He said there was steak, baked potato, and he had even made a salad. In the kitchen, he pulled a plate out of the oven. Then he opened the refrigerator to get the salad out. I had started to pick up the plate of food. I was so hungry! I could not remember the last time I had actually digested food. John slapped my hand. "That's not yours!" he growled. "Oh, sorry." I ducked my head, embarrassed. I opened the oven, but it was empty. Then he said, "Oh, I made you ramen soup. You like that, right?"

"Yeah," I answered. There was a bowl on the counter with some kind of mush in it. I looked at it, stirred it around with a spoon. He had boiled most of the broth away. The noodles had fallen apart, and it was ice-cold. My stomach revolted. No way could I choke that down. I got a beer and went to my spot on the couch. I sat there staring blankly at the TV. Out of the corner of my eye, I saw him fix up his baked potato, put A1 on his steak, dish up some salad, and pour on tons of dressing. I tried to concentrate on the TV show and ignore him. Suddenly, the wall next to my head exploded! Hot bits of potato spattered on my face, the couch, and the floor. I cried out and clawed it off, glaring at John. He had chucked his potato at me from across the room. He was livid. He slammed the plate down on the counter and stalked over. "I slave over a hot stove all fucking night to make *you* a meal and you don't even eat it!" he screamed. "You selfish, spoiled bitch! You don't appreciate *anything* I do for you, do you?" I didn't answer. I just turned back to the TV and chugged some beer.

Earlier in the month, I had tried pretending I didn't care what John did to me, hoping he would leave me alone. It hadn't worked. He knew all my weaknesses and used them against me. I always ended up responding. But now, I was really beginning not to care. It didn't seem to matter what I did or didn't do, the torture was relentless.

Mom's call had made me realize how long it was until July 17. I was sure of only one thing at this point. I wasn't going to be alive when that day came around. I didn't know what, if anything, I could do about that.

John went back to the kitchen for his dinner and brought a glass of Kool-Aid with him. He set the Kool-Aid on the table next to his chair. Within a minute, he had spilled it everywhere. He glared at me like I had spilled it, when it was his own clumsiness from drugs. He sopped it up while I got another beer. John got himself a beer and sat back in his favorite green monstrosity. I couldn't tell if he only pretended to love that chair or if he really couldn't see it as it was. Either way, I didn't care as long as he let me alone about it. Being in the room with John eating was sickening. He smacked, chewed with his mouth open, belched loudly, and talked with food in his mouth. It was disgusting. I tried to ignore him. All I wanted was to suck down as many beers as I could before he started in on me about whatever it was going to be tonight. I did notice he had a steak knife. I briefly wondered where he had hidden all my knives. After I lost my temper, they all disappeared, including the butter knives.

While he ate, he ranted on, spitting out bits of food. I tried not to listen. I knew he was trying to scare me. It usually worked. This time he was saying he was getting bored with how our relationship was going. He wanted to "spice it up, take it to the next level, try new things." He asked what I thought. I didn't respond. He waited a bit for me to answer, then said maybe one day I would "wake up in Las Vegas" with a ring on my finger and a new last name. I didn't like the way he said that at all. Then he laughed, food flying onto his lap. "You really are a SUB if you think I would ever marry you *now!*" he sneered. I don't know if he saw a reaction in my face about Las Vegas. I tried to show no emotion. "The only thing you're good for now is making me money and providing me entertainment. I'm working on ways to combine the two, know what I mean?" he threatened. No response from me.

He dumped his plate in the sink and went to the bedroom for a minute. *Probably hiding the steak knife*, I thought. He came back after getting another beer. We sat for a while with the TV going and him sucking his teeth. I was beyond wondering what I had ever seen in him. I just needed to make it through the moment in front of me, then the next one. John started talking again. He never did appreciate quiet. He asked if I ever wondered what it would be like to have sex with another guy. No response. He laughed cruelly and said, "How do you know you haven't been getting fucked by a dozen guys when you go off to la-la land? It isn't very nice of you to leave me to play by myself, you know!" That got to me! The old John would never have let another guy touch me. But this new one—this demon from hell—I had no idea how far he'd go to degrade me. Somehow, he was aware that I had blackouts. What was I blacking out, if not something too horrible to live through? What type of guy would even enjoy raping an unconscious skeleton covered in wounds, let alone pay John to do it? I decided he had to be yanking my chain, just to get a reaction. It could *not* be true! It was unthinkable, unbearable.

He chuckled. "That got to you, didn't it?" he gloated. He had been watching my face. I was still too easy for him to read. "Now, I haven't started renting you out yet," he said. "I'm still having fun with you myself. So what should we do? Play cards, watch a movie, practice writing prescriptions?" he asked mildly. He had stolen a prescription pad from the hospital before he faked his back injury. He also took a PDR to look up drugs. He worked at forging prescriptions because he couldn't get the doctors to write him large enough ones and he always ran out before he was allowed a refill. He tried to get me to help him. He insisted I should be able to forge a prescription because I had done well in school. I had no clue how he came to that conclusion. But his own attempts weren't good enough to pass at a pharmacy yet.

I got up to get another beer. I still hadn't said a word. John followed me and slapped the fridge shut before I could get a beer. He tried to back me into the cupboards, but I sidestepped and kept moving away. "I am *tired* of this silent treatment!" he raged. "What the *hell* did I ever do to *you?*" That was so absurd, it would have been laughable, if I had the ability to laugh. I felt I would never laugh again. As I moved past the dining table, I saw the PDR, prescription pad, lots of discarded attempts at a decent forgery and the muscle stimulator. Desperately, I wanted to avoid the inevitable. What was left of my spirit rebelled at another night of beatings, mind games, torture, and lessons. But I would *not* forge prescriptions for him, no matter what he did to me! I needed time to think. 21

I turned and ran down the hall to the bedroom, slamming the door as hard as I could. I spun to face the door just as John was coming through it. He had been closer than I thought. Because he always slouched, his head was the first thing across the threshold. The door was closing fast from the hard fling I had given it. I spun just in time to see his face, filled with rage, get squished between the door and the jamb. For some perverse reason, it seemed like the funniest thing I had ever seen. I lost it! I backed up a few steps and broke out with this high-pitched, hysterical, shrieking laugh. It seemed I couldn't stop. John had burst through the door and stormed up to me. He was livid. All I could see was the look on his face, in that instant it had been caught in the door. The look on his face had been so comical! I continued cackling, holding my sides as he began circling me. As I wiped tears from my eyes, I saw two lines: one on each side of his face from the impact of the door. *Good!* I thought. *Now he has a mark from me!*

John started yelling "Shut up, bitch! You think that's funny? You think you can get away with stuff like that? I said, no fighting back! Remember, at the beginning? I'll teach you to laugh at me." He picked me up and threw me across the room. I remember thinking as I flew through the air, "How did this happen to me? How did it get to be like this?" Then I hit the wall. My head hit the bedroom door. My right shoulder and hip hit the wall, but it was my ribs that got it the worst. They crashed into the closet doorknob. I hit the floor and before I could even register the pain or catch my breath, he was there, kicking, screaming, punching me. Thankfully, I blacked out. When I came to, I heard sobbing. It was John. I couldn't cry to save my life. I could barely breathe. As I lay there, hoping to die, I began to make out mumbling and whining mingled with the sobs. "I feel so bad. Why? Why do you make me do it?" John was saying. "I try so hard, but you just won't behave. Hold me. I need you. Come hold me and tell me it's all right. I need you to forgive me!" This was nothing new. He usually bawled after beating me and made me comfort him. Always before, I had crawled over to console him. I know it's sick, but we do what we must to survive. 15

This time, however, I wasn't physically capable of complying. This was the worst I had ever felt. I was sure some of my ribs were at least cracked. It was a struggle just to breathe. "God," I prayed, "let it end." John became aware I wasn't coming to him. He was leaning against the foot of the bed with his head in his hands, just sitting there bawling like a big baby. I was lying on my left side, facing him. I watched him stop and look at me. His face changed. His eyes were black fire, furious. He jumped up and advanced on me. I could not move. "You're just going to *lie* there, selfish bitch!" he screamed. "Can't you see I need some loving attention, some comfort? You always cared more about yourself than *anyone else!* I've *had it* with you!"

"Please," I whispered, "please, kill me!"

"What?" he asked. He crouched close to my face. "Kill you? Put you out of your misery? You dare to ask me for anything? No, I'm still having fun with your sorry ass!" He stood up and kicked me in the stomach. Everything went black.

The next day, I figured John had made me choke down the ramen glop he had made for me. My throat was raw,

I had a nasty taste in my mouth and my stomach felt like it did after lots of heaving. It was my ribs that hurt the most, though. I didn't go to work Tuesday.

Something had changed. Whether it was me or the whole relationship, I didn't know. It was too hard to think, but I knew deep inside, something was different. I didn't shower or even get off the floor. Before, as painful as it had been, I had cleaned myself up, trying as best I could to doctor my new wounds, downing Tylenol to make it to work. I had told myself I needed to keep going for Mark. I couldn't give up. I owed him. It had become a challenge that I had bravely risen to. At least that's what I thought. Now it all seemed meaningless. Time, pain, food, it was all incomprehensible to me. I waited for the end, but the end didn't come.

Shelley did, though. Early Wednesday afternoon, there was a knock on the door. I ignored it. I was lying on the floor, staring out the little bedroom window. John was gone. I'd heard him say something earlier about going out somewhere, but it had been too much effort to listen. *He wouldn't be knocking,* I thought. He has a key. Hell, he has both keys. The knock sounded again. This time I heard someone call out my name. At least, I thought it was my name. What was my name, anyway? Who cares? They called again and said, "I know you're in there! Your manager said you were here!" How did they know I was here, I didn't even know I was here, wherever here was? Then it hit me! I knew that voice! It was Shelley, my best friend! How did she find me?

Oh, God! John would kill her if he found her here! I had to make her go away, fast! I got up and struggled out of my dorm shirt. I don't know how I ended up wearing it, but it showed too much skin. I slipped on jeans and a turtleneck. "Coming!" I called out weakly. I was more stiff and sore than I had ever been in my life. Slowly, I made my way to the door. My heart was pounding, palms sweating. My mind was in a fog. Where had John gone? How long was he going to be? Why didn't I listen? Now I had put Shelley in danger. As I opened the door to let her in, a warning bell went off in my mind, but I couldn't comprehend it. My thoughts were butterflies, flitting around me, never landing and always out of reach.

Shelley came in, looking at me closely. "God, Jenny, you look awful! How much weight have you lost?" she exclaimed. My stomach was burning. Before I could answer, I clapped my hand on my mouth and headed to the bathroom. All that came up was stomach acid, but getting it up was excruciating. Shelley sat on the tub next to me, terribly worried. It occurred to me she was talking. She was saying Mom had been worried because I had missed work and her phone call. Shelley and I had been through a lot together. We were more like sisters than friends. She even called my mom, "Mom." There had been no secrets between us until John came along. But I was frantic to get her *out* before John came home. She was still talking about how Mom didn't know where I lived. I remember telling Shelley the general area of our apartment. She said she had gone to every complex in the area, asking about me. This was taking way too long. Why was she here? I had to get her out! She was in danger. Every time I tried to get up, I retched again. Nothing was coming up and I was too weak to rise. 3

"I'm fine," I croaked out. "Please, you have to go."

"You are anything, but fine." she stated. "Has Mom seen you? Of course not. That's why she's worried."

"Please," I begged, "just go. I'll call Mom tonight at work. I promise." I told her I couldn't talk. I had to get ready for work. The seconds seemed to race past. I imagined John's footfalls outside. God! Why wouldn't she just go? Couldn't she see I was a lost cause? "Go, go, go!" I wanted to scream at her. But I couldn't take that deep of a breath. She helped me to the couch. "Jenny, you need to go to the doctor. Where are your shoes?" she asked. An image sprang into my mind: the end of a shotgun barrel, John threatening to kill all my loved ones. "No, really, I'm fine." I said. "Just had the flu is all. John went to get some medicine. He'll be upset if he comes back and I'm not in bed." I just said whatever popped into my head, whether it made sense or not. She had to go! I couldn't take it if he did anything to her because I was too stupid to get her away safely. "You promise you'll call Mom?" she asked.

"Yes, I will," I replied. "She's taking me for Chinese for my birthday. Everything is fine." She stared at me for a while. My heart raced, mind frozen. I had tried my best, my pitiful, not-good-enough best, to make her leave, keep her safe, but as usual, I failed. Someone smart would have known what to say, would have been convincing, so she could leave and live. But I was a SUB. A SUB couldn't talk right, couldn't *think*, and now Shelley had to die. And I knew I would have to watch it. All this ran through my mind while she stared at me. Finally, she said, "If you don't call Mom tonight, I'm going to bring her and Dad here to get you." It sounded like a threat, a terrible, deadly threat. Only it would be Mom, Dad, and Shelley who would die, while I, who wanted to die, would have to watch and still live. "Okay." I tried to smile. She leaned down to kiss my forehead. "Take a shower, lady, you'll feel better," she said. Then she was gone. A shower? Oh, yeah, I'm sure I smelled. What day was it? I had to get to work. But John wasn't here. I had no key to unlock the door. Damn him! I hated him! Sometimes, I had to dig through his pockets looking for the key to let myself out, while he slept peacefully. But he wasn't here. There were no pockets to look through. I would miss another day. Probably get fired. So what? Then what good would I be? John would have to kill me, I reasoned. Tippy jumped up on the couch, purring. He started mewing and rubbing his head on me. Ken hopped around in his cage. John's bunny hopped by. I was just another animal in the zoo. Trapped, caged, and not even fed by the zookeeper. Fed? When did the kitty eat last? Slowly, I got up. His dishes were empty. I gave him food and water, fed Ken and the rabbit. It was after 2:00 p.m. I needed to get to the bus stop or I would be late for work. Did I want to go to work? I didn't know, but habit took over. I put on shoes and got my purse. When the latch clicked behind me, I froze. All that time, I had been in an *unlocked* apartment! I could have left at any time! What the hell was going on?

I was leaving now, without John's permission. In a daze, I hurried to the bus stop as fast as my battered body would go. On the ride, my mind continued to jump from one random thought to another. Had Shelley really come? Would John know she had been there? Why had he left the door unlocked? It was a test! It had to be.

Had I failed or passed? Who could say? I didn't know the rules. Rules? Oh, the lessons. I'm Jennifer, I'm ugly, I'm fat, I'm stupid, I'm worthless, I'm useless, I talk too much, no one loves me but John, no one will ever love me like John. I remember now. It was comforting to repeat the familiar words. It soothed me so much I almost missed my stop. It had been a few days since we had done the lessons, I thought. We need to go over them more often. I always forget. What day was it again?

At work, everyone thought I should still be home in bed. "We don't want to get what you have," they said. *Don't worry*, I thought, *it's not catching!* They kept their distance to be safe from germs. Or was that because I smelled bad? No, it's because you're a SUB! Stupid SUB, don't you know anything? No one *really* likes you, they just pretend, to be nice. They're so nice. Everyone's nice, but you. You are selfish. Thoughts raced through my mind, but none stayed very long. I drank loads of coffee and kept to myself. At dinner break, I called Mom. Yes, I was feeling better. Yes, I could go to lunch. Okay, I would meet her at noon on Friday. No, I didn't need a ride. Back to work. The night raced by and then John was there to get me.

He had the biggest smile on his face. Like the big bad wolf! Oh! I've made him happy! Yeah! No, wait. I don't like him, he's mean to me. There is something I need to remember, something important. "I called Mom," I said. No, that's not it. There was a test. A test! A trap! The door wasn't locked. I left without permission. This is bad, really bad! What? He was yelling, "Did you hear anything I said?" he asked.

"Sorry, I'm really tired from work," I answered.

"I fail to see how you can get tired sitting on your fat ass, gossiping all night!" he said, sarcastically. "You don't talk about me, do you?"

"Only about how sweet you are all the time," I said.

"Okay, now don't distract me from my news again. I have a surprise for you—a birthday surprise!" he exclaimed.

Nooooo! I thought. "But my birthday isn't until Sunday," I said.

"I know when your birthday is, stupid," he snapped. "Are you ready for the news?" I nodded. "You are going on a field trip!" he announced. I stared at him blankly. "I told the next-door neighbor you would go to church with her. Won't that be nice?" he grinned. I was dumbfounded. Church? I knew she was Catholic, like John. I was not. I had absolutely no interest in attending Mass, ever. Certainly not on my birthday with a complete stranger. I had barely spoken to any of the neighbors. I didn't even know this lady's name! "I don't want to go to church!" I said. 18, 25

"Sure you do. It will be good for you," he replied.

"No," I said. "It's my birthday. I don't want to get up early on a work day and go to Mass. I'm not even Catholic." John slammed on the brakes. The drink he had brought me sloshed out. I heard horns and squealing tires behind us. I noticed some undissolved powder swirling in the bottom of my glass. He was screaming in my face, spraying spit, while cars sped around us, blaring their horns. "Now look what you've done, shithead!" he fumed. "I go to all the trouble to bring you a relaxing drink and you spill it all over! I don't know why I even bother trying to be nice to you!"

"Neither do I. So why don't you just kill me and get it over with!" I said.

"Oh, you don't get to mess up my plans that way," he replied, gunning the engine. He jabbed me in the ribs with his elbow. I gasped, but was grateful it wasn't my right side. 1

I couldn't think of a place on my body that didn't hurt. I couldn't think of a time when I hadn't hurt. My feet, butt, and what was left of my breasts had peeled some. I had given up wearing bras because of the pain. I didn't have hardly any breasts left. Before we moved in, I had been a B cup. Now I doubted I would fill an A. I had so many nasty words cut into me, in various stages of healing. John had started cutting them in places that would be the most uncomfortable. Like my armpits, so deodorant would sting. Another favorite place of his was where my thighs and crotch met, so underwear irritated them. He still enjoyed biting, kicking, and dragging me. I had carpet burns and what I was sure were cigarette and match burns in intimate places. All that on top of numerous footprint-shaped bruises made a sickening display. I had stopped looking in mirrors, except when we recited the lessons. That was okay since he didn't hit me in the face.

We didn't say another word until we got back to the apartment. "Finish your drink," he commanded. I did, powder and all. After we got upstairs and were safely locked in, he told me if I didn't want to go to church, I had to tell the neighbor myself. Things were so off.

He never let me talk to the neighbors or the manager. "She's trying to be nice to you, to reach out to you. If you don't appreciate her generosity, you are going to say so to her face!" he spat. "I'm not telling her how selfish and ungrateful you are!"

I just headed to the fridge for a beer. That's all I wanted. I didn't see him stick his foot out. The next thing I knew, I was face down on the floor. Lights swam in my vision. I could hear his laughter. "Get me a beer, too," he said, "when you manage to get your lazy, fat ass up!" It was a long night. Something nagged at the edge of my mind. It was frustrating. I was on my guard and couldn't remember why. It was like a trap had been set, I had stepped into it, but it hadn't sprung. Why? What was he waiting for? What had I even done? Maybe it was just what he had drugged me with or my imagination. My thoughts were incoherent and disjointed when I could even grasp them.

Then it was Thursday, payday again. This Saturday, it would be one month since we moved in. One month of pure hell! Tomorrow, we would go to the bank, cash my check, and John would drop me off at the restaurant to have lunch with my mom. He had not beaten me last night as far as I could tell. He had made me strip and endure his inspection. He circled me, ticking off my many flaws, but not finding any spots without injury, he said we could skip a beating. There had been no rape either. Maybe he just couldn't get it up or had been with someone else. Maybe I just looked too gross anymore for him to want me. I didn't care. I just drank until I passed out. So I had a bad hangover and an even worse feeling in

my soul. Like there had been a shift in the universe. I felt
the terrible truth of it, but couldn't explain it.

That night at work, it hit me like a ton of bricks. I
had left! I had not been punished for it! He hadn't said
a word about it! Did he know Shelley had been there? I
was so unobservant, he could have been watching from
the courtyard and I wouldn't have noticed. Did he forget
to lock the door? How could he? He never forgot! He
had taken the phone. Why would he have left the door
unlocked? Even though I hadn't run away or told on him,
I still knew that punishment was coming. Punishment
was always coming. By the time John picked me up, I was
shaking inside from head to toe.

He didn't seem to notice. We went home, I opened a
beer and sat in my spot. John was being cordial. I was on
guard. John got a beer, sat in his chair, and asked what
I was wearing for my date with Mom. "Are my favorite
jeans still in the laundry?" I asked. I hadn't seen them since
his parents came for dinner. Was that only a week ago?
"You mean your pee pants?" he asked. My face flushed,
remembering. "You are going to wear pee pants to lunch
with your mommy?" he said derisively.

"They will be clean once they're washed. Where are
they?" I asked.

"I threw them away, idiot!" John yelled. "I'm not
washing *my* clothes with your pee pants!" We went
through the lessons again that night. I no longer resisted
them. It was too much effort to fight. Then surprisingly,
he told me to go to bed. "You have a big day tomorrow,"
he said.

"Just lunch with Mom," I replied.

"No, you have a babysitting job Friday night.," he told me. This was the first I heard of any babysitting job. Seems he was going out with the neighbors and I was going to watch their daughter. I went to bed, but didn't sleep much. John's rabbit had made a nest in the box spring and I could hear her rustling around. Plus, I kept waiting for him to come in and do something. I lay there, curled in a ball on my left side, tense and stiff. I would drift off, jerk awake, and almost fall off my twelve inches of bed space. Finally, I took a blanket and lay on the floor between the bed and wall. Tippy curled up with me, purring contentedly.

On Friday, John said I couldn't have breakfast. He needed to shop after we cashed my check and there wasn't much to eat. Since I was having a big lunch, I could wait. I made coffee and took a long shower. It felt really good. I was healing, turning all bluish-yellowish-green, kind of like a rotting corpse. But I wasn't in as much pain now. Mostly the ribs on my right where the doorknob made contact and my hip joints were sore. I actually thought maybe the worst was over. He had gotten over his anger, had his fun and we'd ride out the next two months. Then just part ways. Who was I kidding? No one. I knew this was just the calm before the next storm. I wondered how many times I could do this. Get beaten and tortured nearly to death, only to get a short break and start all over again. I didn't know. I didn't want to find out either, but I knew I would.

After the bank, John dropped me off by the restaurant with a dark warning look. Mom's car was there. I slid into a booth across from her. That was the most uncomfortable hour I'd ever spent with my mom. She wasn't happy about my obvious weight loss. I had picked a bulky sweater to wear, but it didn't fool her. It did keep me warm though. Phoenix in May is far from cool, but it seemed I was always cold. "I noticed you came and got Ken. I thought you were leaving him with us," she said. No mention of all the meat we stole. "John wanted him," I replied. We went through the buffet, but I found I could not eat much. My stomach rebelled. I didn't want to push it and have Mom see me gagging. I took small bites, chewing slowly. When it was almost time to go, she slid a card across the table. I opened it. Inside was fifty dollars. I almost cried. Wow! I hadn't cried in a while. I didn't think I still could. "I don't want you to spend a penny of that on John!" she said.

"I won't," I promised. In my purse, the lining was torn at the bottom. I slipped the money between the lining and outside. Then I tucked the card in. John's car was in the parking lot, idling.

"Mom, I have to go. John is here. He did the grocery shopping. I don't want the ice cream to melt." That was the most I'd said the whole hour. We hugged. I swear she gasped and had tears in her eyes. I know I had tears in mine. John insisted on looking at the card before he left the parking lot. "No money! No present?" he accused.

"The lunch was the present," I lied. We drove back and put away the groceries. Then we played "How many punches does it take to…" Well, you get the idea. It took only two. 22

After the game came another round of lessons. Then he insisted on my trying to forge prescriptions. I messed some up on purpose. He shoved me out of the chair, saying I was hopeless and good for nothing. I spent the rest of the afternoon cleaning. The place was a mess and I would be babysitting at our apartment. I didn't want them to see it like that.

John told me to think about what I really wanted for my birthday while he was out. I had no idea what that meant! Could I ask him to get rid of the ugly green chair? Tell him to kill himself? Make him let me go? I didn't think any of those would really happen.

The neighbors came and gave instructions for bedtime. The little girl had brought her pajamas and some games. She had already eaten dinner. She had a package of Jiffy Pop for later. John gave me a look that I understood only too well. We would be playing the "how many..." game again when he got home. They left and we turned on the TV. We couldn't find anything she wanted to watch, so we played checkers. I got beat six games in a row by a six-year-old and I wasn't letting her win! I couldn't concentrate. We made the popcorn, then played with Tippy. I showed her how Ken liked to take a shower in the kitchen sink. She asked if Ken and Tippy ever played together. I panicked, thinking my popcorn was going to come up. "No, of course not," I said. "Ken is a bird, Tippy is a kitty. It's time for bed." She brushed her teeth and I tucked her in on my side of the bed.

Then I started drinking fast, one beer after another, mindlessly watching whatever flickered on the TV. About an hour later, I remembered the money Mom gave me. I fished it out of my purse. I had a small stand in the bedroom for personal stuff. It was just a homemade wooden box really. But in the very back where the top and sides came together was a crack. I folded the fifty dollar bill and slid it into that crack. Then I stood looking at the box from every angle. The money wasn't visible.

I went back to the living room and started to drink again. They got home about 1:30 a.m. The dad scooped up his daughter and John followed him out to open doors for him. The mom and I gathered up her stuff. She gave me twenty dollars. I protested and she insisted. "Get yourself something pretty with it," she said and winked as she left. "What did that mean?" I wondered. Did John know she was going to pay me? I would have to give the money to him. Fast as I could, I went to the bedroom and crammed the twenty in with the fifty. Just in time, I was seated in my spot, beer in hand, Tippy on my lap. My heart was beating so wildly. I tried to breathe slowly and look calm. Did he know? Did my face betray me?

"Well," he said, "I told you it was going to be a *big* day, didn't I?"

"Yes, you called it right," I answered. "You always know these things."

"Trap, trap, trap!" my mind was screaming.

Nearly 33 percent of women killed in US workplaces between 2003–2008 were killed by a current or former intimate partner.[3]

PART 3

Dying in the Pits

"Of course I called it, SUB! I'm the *man!* I'm smart," he crowed. "Now the question is, why does a handsome, smart guy like me put up with a loser like you?" My mind was shrieking "trap!" so loudly, I almost said it out loud. Instead, I said, "Because you love me?"

"And why do I love you?" he asked quietly. I thought and thought, panicked, terrified. The ax was going to fall. This was quicksand, stranded in the ocean during a hurricane, no way out. The wrong answer would seal my doom. Then I remembered my doom was already sealed. I hung my head and whispered, "I don't know."

"That's right," he answered. "That's the big mystery of the universe. No one knows why a popular, handsome stud like me would give a second look at a piece of shit like *you!*" He was shouting now.

He advanced on me. "How much?" he asked.

"What?" I answered. He frowned.

"How much did I make tonight?" he yelled.

"I don't understand," I replied. "What are you talking about?"

"Damn, you are slow, SUB!" he ground out. "How much money did I get for babysitting?" He spit each word at me.

"I, uh, what? There's no money. Why would you ask that?" I stammered. My heart was hammering so fast. Did the neighbor tell John she paid me? If I lied about the amount, would he know I was lying? He stood there glaring at me. "Why would you get paid anyway?" I asked, stalling. "I'm the one who babysat."

"Well, I got you the job, SUB!" he gloated. "I'm the one who told them how much you love kids, how good you are with them. I deserve something, don't you think?" he asked.

"Sure, if I got paid I would share it with you," I replied. "Don't I always give you my money?" Big mistake! The trap snapped shut. I was caught fast. "That's it!" he screamed. "See, it's still all about you! Selfish, fucking SUB! 'My money!'" he mimicked me. "It is *our* money! Everything is *ours!* You have *nothing!*" He ran over and grabbed the muscle stimulator. I was frozen in place. He came over, yanked me off the couch, and pulled me down the hall. His silence was ominous. 22

In the bedroom, he slammed me face first into the wall. He pressed himself against me, so I couldn't get away. Reaching down, he jerked my jeans and underwear down. He pushed me up higher on the wall, so my feet were hanging. "I'm going to teach you some manners, some simple appreciation for me and all I do for you, fucking, selfish bitch!" he growled in my ear. He jammed the stimulator into my crotch. It had been made so it gave mild intermittent pulses of electricity. John had altered it to give a continuous jolt that was a lot stronger than before. He shoved it hard into my private places, keeping me pinned to the wall with his upper body. My feet kicked aimlessly while I made awful gurgling noises. It seemed to go on forever. When it stopped, I wondered how it didn't seem to affect John. If he is pressed against me, shouldn't he be getting shocked too? I thought. Then it started again. Over and over, he shocked me. Digging it into me, trying to rape me with the stimulator it seemed.

Finally, it stopped. We both fell to the floor. I felt weak, drained, and tingly. My legs were like wet noodles. John rolled over and found the stimulator. Apparently, it was bloody. "Oh, great!" he spat out, disgusted. "Are you still on the rag, SUB? Why the *hell* don't you tell me these things?" I had very irregular periods. It was common for me to be on my period for ten days or longer. But again, I knew this blood wasn't from my period. I prayed, "God, please don't let me be pregnant!"

"I guess I have to alter my plans for tonight," John said. We went through the lessons. Then he had me pick a paper from his hand for either "punishment" or "loving." The paper I chose said "punishment." He laughed and showed me the other paper. It also said "punishment." "You really don't actually think you'd get loving when you're all nasty, do you?" he chuckled. Either way, it didn't matter to me. Sex with him was a punishment. Most of the time when he made me choose, he ended up giving me both. There was always some stupid excuse why.

He told me to get dressed. The lessons had been conducted with me still on the floor, half naked. I shakily pulled on my panties and jeans. I still felt weird, all jerky and weak. We went to the table in the dining area. He demanded I write prescriptions for him. I refused. He grabbed his bunny and threatened to kill her. Still, I refused. He threw her across the room. She sped into the bedroom. I rarely saw her after that. He got Ken out and threatened to feed him to Tippy. I wrote, but with my fingers shaking, the results weren't to John's satisfaction. He grabbed my hair, jerked me off the chair, dragging me across the carpet. I blacked out. [19,20]

Saturday morning, John acted like everything was great. He brought me coffee. I woke up on the couch. "Did I sleep here?" I wondered. "Why would he let me get away with that?" I could tell he had gone through my purse when I got my cigarettes out. He was probably looking for the babysitting money. I didn't say anything about it. "Don't forget, dear SUB," he said. "You need to tell the neighbor you aren't going to church with her, unless you changed your mind."

"No, I haven't changed it. I'm not going," I replied. I finished my coffee and went to take a shower. The insides of my thighs were cut and bruised. I had new bite and burn marks to go with the new shoe print bruises. I dressed in clothes that were falling off me, wondering, "How long can I last?"

I did my chores in silence: feeding the pets, cleaning out the litter box and Ken's cage. Just before noon, I asked when John was going to let me go next door. "Whenever you're ready," he answered. He unlocked the door and made a show of opening it wide, bowing and letting me pass by. He stood just inside our apartment, watching me as I knocked. I knew if I ran, he'd be on me in two steps. The neighbor answered and I told her I wasn't going to church tomorrow. I said it was a work day for me and I needed to sleep. She said she understood, and if I changed my mind, I was welcome to go with her anytime. I went back into our apartment and John locked the door. Later, he left to do laundry. I sat at the bedroom window, smoking and petting Tippy.

When the laundry was finished, John asked me what I wanted to do that night. I looked at him blankly. "Remember," he smiled, "I told you to think about what you really wanted for your birthday?" I just stared past him. Maybe if I pretended hard enough, it would be like he really wasn't there. He was talking again, "I figured you'd like to go out tonight since you have to work tomorrow," he was saying. Go out? Where? With him, like on a date? What was he talking about? "You're going to need to get ready soon," he said and turned away. "Oh yeah," he added as he walked away, "I invited someone to go with us. I hope you don't mind. He's cool. He's a new friend. You haven't met him yet, but I think you'll like him." John left the room and I was left swimming in my jumbled thoughts. 18

Sometimes when we had been out with friends, his friends, rarely ever mine, he would make me dance with someone. I would protest, but eventually, I always ended up doing what John wanted me to. Then he would accuse me of enjoying it too much, of liking the other guy more than him. It always turned into a fight that I couldn't win. Vaguely, I remembered John saying something about thinking of what I "really" wanted for my birthday. Obviously, I had taken too long to think of something, so he picked for me. Not that he would have let me do what I chose anyway. It was just another of his ways of yanking my chain. *I don't care*, I thought, "I just don't care about anything."

John came back in the room a few hours later. He picked out clothes for both of us and left to shower and dress. Still, I didn't move. "Come on, get moving!" he said, "Our friend will be here soon. I have a special night planned for us!" Mechanically, I dressed and left the bedroom. I curled up on the couch, waiting. "Aren't you gonna curl your hair or anything?" John asked.

"No, it takes too long," I replied.

"Oh well," he said, "I guess it's your birthday night, but I told this guy you are really hot. I thought you'd want to make a good first impression."

Yeah, so you can beat me for it later," I thought to myself. *No thanks, I'll pass.*

There was a knock on the door. John jumped up and let him in. *So here's the guy John is going to sell me to*, I thought. He wasn't very good looking. Like John, he was tall and dark, but not as skinny. "Was that on purpose or coincidence? Who cares? It doesn't matter. Just get through this." I was becoming pretty numb. John introduced us. I promptly forgot his name. I really did not believe we were going out. I hadn't been anywhere besides work for so long. The lunch with Mom seemed like a dream. I almost got up to check on the money she gave me to see if it was real. But John would find it, I reasoned. It's not there anyway. None of that really happened. None of that money exists except in my head.

I was in my own world and had missed the guys' conversation. "SUB!" John called out. "Hey! SUB, baby, I'm talking to you! Where you at?" he questioned.

"Oh, sorry, what did you say?" I answered.

"I got some great drugs here for our special night. I think you'll like them. They won't make you sick like the other ones do. How many do you want?" he asked.

"Trap! Trap! Trap!" my mind screamed. So he's asking now, instead of sneaking them in my drink! He even admitted they made me sick. That had to be for "friend's" benefit, to show how caring and concerned John was about me. But he didn't ask "do you want any?" He asked "how many?" I had to take at least one or John would be slighted in front of his new best friend. That would mean trouble for me. No choice here! I can't refuse them without incurring the wrath of John. God! What hell would these pills put me in? Even if I refuse and take the punishment for making him look bad, he'll just crush them up and put them in my drink. No way am I not drinking! I need something to get me through this night!

John had walked up and was leaning over me. I could see in his eyes, he was mad, but trying not to show it. "How many?" he asked again. Oh, was I taking too long to decide as usual? "Just one please," I answered sweetly. Maybe one wouldn't do too much damage. But then again, maybe six would put me out of my misery for good! With as little as I now weighed and mixing them with alcohol, this could be my way out! But deep down, I knew John wouldn't give me that many. He looked up all his pills in the PDR. He would know what a lethal dose was. He came back with a beer and handed me a pill to take. With both guys watching, I swallowed the pill, taking several swigs of beer to wash it down. John handed Friend a beer and sat in his ugly chair. Friend sat next to me on the couch, but not too close. We watched TV while we drank. I was a ball of nerves. I wanted to get drunk and black out. "Please don't make me be conscious for this!" I begged God. I got up to open another beer and John stopped me. "Whoa, slow down, birthday girl!" he said. "We're going out, remember?"

And we did! We drove to a nightclub, not one of John's regular bars. Looking back, I realize that people we knew would have seen how bad I looked compared to before. There would have been questions. But John explained it as wanting to show me a good time for my birthday. We danced and drank. Whatever that pill was, it didn't seem to affect me negatively. John was really high, all goofy, and full of grins. I danced with Friend, but no slow dances. We played pool, badly. We were too messed up to be any good. I passed out in the car on the way back. I don't remember anything and I don't want to remember.

I was in my pajamas, curled up on the couch in the morning with a bad hangover. It took a lot of coffee and Tylenol to get me ready for work. Nothing was said about the previous night by either of us. Friend had not been there when I woke up. John had been passed out on the bed. No one wished me Happy Birthday at work. I did my job and John picked me up when it was time. Back at the apartment, we played "How many punches…" It only took one and all that came up was coffee. "Just checking,"

John said. "You might have had cake and ice cream or gone out to dinner. We both know how sneaky you are, SUB." 21

"I have a new game!" he suddenly announced. "It's called Chicken kung-fu and if you win, I'll tell you about last night." I just sat in my place, nursing a beer. No response. John reached for my beer and I flinched. "Ha! You already lost!" he exclaimed. "But I guess that wasn't fair. I didn't say we started and you don't know the rules." He took my beer, sat me on the floor in the bedroom, and stood close to me. He explained that he was going to walk around me, and at any time, he could kick out toward me. If I moved, blinked, or flinched, I lost. Every time I lost, he would get to punish me. If I won, he promised to fill me in on all the gory details of last night, after we got back from the club. I already hated this game and it hadn't even started yet. Win or lose, it was punishment for me all the way.

I lost. I lost again. "Come on, SUB!" John protested, "It's not that hard. You aren't even trying! Concentrate, SUB!" He circled me, suddenly kicked out, knocking me over. "Oh, no, I'm not loving you, no matter how much you beg me!" he said. "And you did beg last night. You know that? You begged, SUB. Would you like me to tell you? Huh? Do you want to hear all about it?" No answer. He snapped and started pummeling me with his fists. "Answer me, SUB!" he screamed. "Tell me you want to know! What does it take to get through to you, bitch?" I wouldn't know, I blacked out. 21

The rest of that week went pretty much the same way. Each day, I woke up on the couch, sometimes in pajamas, sometimes naked. I kept a blanket folded up and tucked under the end, where the table and couch met. Sometimes, I was covered by it and sometimes not. Tippy was always curled up next to me. John continued to torment me about what had supposedly happened with his friend. I never saw the guy again and I could not believe John. Sometimes, he described an orgy that he said I was a willing participant in, then laughed and said, "Naw, that didn't happen." I had been so messed up by the stimulator, I really couldn't tell if I had been used. "Surely I would know if something had happened!" I reasoned. And John would not have raped me that night. He still thought I was on my period. But the truth was—I didn't care. I couldn't care. Because caring took emotion, effort, energy. Precious energy that I needed just to survive another hour, another day. I couldn't waste energy on stupid things like caring what happened to me.

By Friday morning, I was pretty docile. John had tried to get a response out of me all week. I had gone through a "pretend not to care" phase earlier, but he had always managed to get a response, eventually. Now the only response he ever got was me begging him to kill me. I remember lying on the floor, begging him, "Just kill me, please. Get it over with. You win! I can't take anymore!" Always, he replied he was still having fun. I couldn't even comprehend what "fun" was anymore. Had I ever had this mysterious "fun"?

The crystal glasses were all gone. He had broken the last one a couple nights ago. I can't tell you what he wrote on my butt with it because I never bothered to look at it. I had nothing left. There was not a part of me he hadn't picked apart, shredded, stomped on, destroyed, and mocked into nonexistence.

In the afternoon, he made me go to the bedroom. He said he couldn't *work* with me sitting on the couch, glaring at him. Ha! I didn't even see him as I sat there staring into space. I started to sit by the window and he said, "No!" He made me strip and get on my side of the bed. He tried to have sex with me. I reached over and picked up a nail file. I started to file my nails, figuring at least I could get something worthwhile done. He lost his erection, beat me, and slammed out of the room. I dressed and lay back down. Later, the little neighbor girl came in. She had come over to play with Tippy and Ken. John had sent her to get me up. But I didn't get up. I remember her sitting next to me for a while, talking. I have no idea what she said. Finally, she asked me something. I said, "I'm just sitting here watching the wheels go round and round. I really love to watch them roll." She didn't understand. I guess she wasn't familiar with John Lennon. She left and I kept watching the wheels dance and play on the wall.

That night, John rousted me and we stayed up drinking and playing his games. Saturday, he said he had made a decision. I needed to get my priorities straight. He wasn't having much fun anymore. I wasn't "playing right." He felt I had lost sight of why I was there. Didn't I care what happened to Mark? Was I really giving up, so soon? Was I really that selfish to leave Marky alone in this fight? He said I was a fool and very much wrong if I thought he would back off my brother just because I died. So he told me to take a walk and think about it. He sent me out to a field that he could see from the balcony. It was kitty-corner to the apartment complex.

I walked in a daze. There was a good-sized rock in the field. I sat down on it. So tired! What was I here for again? I looked up. There was John, standing on the walkway in front of our door. He was leaning on the railing. I could feel his hateful glare. What did he even want from me? Oh yeah, some guy named Marky. He's probably going to sell me to him next. So what? It doesn't matter. Nothing matters. Why the hell am I here? "Think about Marky," he said. Who's Marky? That kid on the Life commercial? I don't care about him! I don't even know him! John certainly doesn't know him. How can he hurt that kid?

Hey! I'm outside! I could run! John's far away. He couldn't catch me before I got to a house. Got some help. What help? No one has helped you. No one will. All the screaming and fighting and no one has called the cops or come to the door to check on you. Idiot! If you run, John will destroy Mark. Mark! Who is this Mark guy everyone is talking about? The voices in my head were starting to take over more and more. I had no idea which thoughts were mine and which weren't. Then I saw his face! Right there in front of me. My brother! My loving, precious big brother. Tears started flowing down my face. Memories flooded my mind. I was no longer sitting on a rock in a field being watched by a psychopath. I was reliving moment after moment with my brother and the rest of my family. Birthdays, Christmases, snow days off from school, summer vacations, road trips. I felt the force of their love, the acceptance they gave so freely. This was why I was here. This was what I was fighting for. To keep John focused on me, so they could live a "John-free" life!

For the first time, I noticed the sun. It felt so warm on my face. John was still there, watching. He'd said I could have an hour. How long had I been here? I did not want to go back. It would be like walking straight into the pits of *hell*. But I had to go. I had no choice if I wanted my family safe. Just a few more weeks and Mark would be married. I had to give him that! I owed him that much, at least. I would miss his wedding and he would never know that this was my wedding gift to him: keeping John from messing up his life more than he already had. I could do it! I had to! I was nearly halfway there. Surely, John would let up a bit. He did before when he saw it was too much. He had backed off and given me time to heal, to regroup. After all, his goal was to go all the way to July 17. At this rate, I wouldn't make it that long. He had to back off, so he could keep playing his sick, demented games. I stood up and slowly walked back. I felt John's black, demon eyes on me the whole time.

I walked across the courtyard, glanced at the pool I had never so much as dipped a toe in, went past Barb's apartment. She said, "Hi!" I just kept on going, past the laundry room, up the stairs, around the corner and all the way to the end: the end of the walkway, the end of freedom, the end of me. The end of this *hell*? Would I find heaven at the end of this hell?

I had been raised in church until we moved to Phoenix. My parents stopped going after the move. They had what was to them a logical reason, but they didn't share it with us kids. I thought they were hypocrites. After we moved, I played the part of "good girl" all week. Going to school, doing my homework and chores, but on the weekends, I partied with a set of friends my parents hadn't met. I had rebelled big time! It's a funny thing about rebellion. You think you're making your own decisions, standing up for yourself against whatever it is you are rebelling against. But in reality, you are allowing Satan to control you. Oh, he lets you think you are in control, but you aren't. It seemed like Satan and John were the same person. It was only a matter of time before my sins caught up to me. Sin will always find you out. It will always be revealed. It will always trap you because it *is* a trap!

I had gone to church a couple of times with a friend from high school, but praying, reading my Bible, seeking God's will, I rejected all that help. I was doing it on my own! Yeah, and look where it got me! I knew I was saved. I had heard the Gospel and accepted Christ as my Savior in the fifth grade. I knew heaven was my destination when I died. But now I could see that I had wasted the time he had given me. Did I tell anyone in high school that Jesus loved them? No. I had nothing to show for my time on earth. I was a waste of life, of breath, of space.

God could change that though. He can do all things. I just had to let him have control again. The second I cried out for help, he would take over and win the battle for me. But I'm stubborn and prideful. I got myself into this mess, I should have to get myself out. Besides, I've messed up so badly, he shouldn't even want me anymore! At least, that's what the voices in my head were telling me. So I decided it was up to me to fix this. Thinking was a difficult task for me anymore. I don't know if it was hunger, all the head slamming I endured, or the lessons and games, but my brain didn't seem to function well.

Simple things like getting dressed, lighting a cigarette, or taking a shower were monumental tasks. I had to concentrate hard to remember the order of how they were accomplished. Did I do that part already? Sometimes, I tried to put on socks when I was already wearing them. Then I had to think, are the ones on my feet clean or dirty? I couldn't remember. It was so easy to just drink beer after beer. That I could do without too much effort.

John was waiting for me at the end of the walkway. The apartment door was open. We stood facing each other for a couple seconds and then he gestured for me to enter first. I turned and stepped over the threshold. I heard the door close, the bolt slide home, locking me in. John was on me in an instant. He tackled me to the floor and kept me pinned down. He sneered in my ear, "That's right. *I always win!* It's my way or the highway!" I waited. He continued, "Are you ready to get started? I thought of some great games while you were on your walk." I waited. "Come on, SUB, answer me!" he demanded. "It's no fun to play alone! Maybe when the games are over, we can take a trip!" he ventured. "I've been promising you a trip, haven't I? Wouldn't it be nice to just get away!" Still no answer from me. 27

He jumped up and kicked me in the lower abdomen. He was screaming and pacing, kicking out at me to accent a word here and there. "This is *not* how you play! You are supposed to cooperate, play with me. I feel so alone! So *bad!* Don't you care about me at all? You came back to me! You *have* to care, SUB. You just have to! I try and try, but you won't play. Why?" He was sobbing. "Why are you so mean and selfish to me? I try as hard as I can."

Suddenly, he dropped to the floor next to me. We lay there, face-to-face. His eyes were black fire, burning into me. I imagined they would be the last thing I saw when I died. Then he spoke again, "I love you so much! Do you know that? No one could love you more than me!" I had no response. I knew a major beating was coming. I was trying to prepare for it, conserve energy. I couldn't afford to get involved in his head games. Why did he always have to have a reaction from me? I wondered. "Just get it over with so I can go drink!" I begged silently. 21

John had let me out. He had given me the chance to strengthen my resolve. Now it seemed he was determined to snatch that resolve away as soon as I had found it. He rolled on top of me. His face was right in mine, nose to nose. His eyes blazed hatred, fury, meanness. "You whore!" he breathed out. "You disgusting, fucking whore! You weren't a virgin when we met! You'd already given it to your Marky! To your dad! You will pay for your lies!" By now, he was yelling. He took hold of my hair on both sides of my head. He mashed his face into mine, noses squashed together, his lips spraying spit, our eyes almost touching. "What do you *want* from me?" he ground out. "I have given you *everything!* Still, you aren't satisfied!" He sat up, still holding my hair. "Answer me!" he demanded and slammed my head into the floor. I saw stars, but stayed silent. "You will answer me *now!*" he raged and slammed my head again. The edges of my vision blurred and went dark. I felt sick to my stomach, but still I stayed silent. 24

John disentangled his hands, grabbed my feet, and headed for the bedroom. He dropped my legs and closed the door. It occurred to me that he almost always closed the door. *I wonder why?* I thought. *It's not like anyone could see into the bedroom from the living room windows.* He pulled a belt out of a drawer and circled me with it. I could hear him dragging the belt, the buckle clinking as it bounced on the carpet. I kept my eyes closed, waiting, barely breathing. Swack! The belt struck me across the thighs. "You just love to be punished, don't you, whore?" he snarled. "You think you're better than me, smarter than me! Well, you're not!" Over and over, he whipped me with the belt, the buckle digging in. I curled up and rolled over. He kicked me and stomped on me until the blackness took me away.

I came back to reality later that afternoon. It was quiet. I couldn't believe how badly I hurt. I was on the floor in the corner by the window. Slowly, I tried moving. My skin was on fire in places with welts and gouges from the belt buckle. The wounds from the first belt attack were finally mostly healed and now this! I slowly moved around until I could see out the window. John's car wasn't in his spot, but that didn't mean he was gone. Half the time he didn't park in his place. My ribs had taken some kicks and it was painful to breathe, like it had been after he had thrown me across the room. All the resolve I'd had earlier was gone. I realized that I was not going to make it to July 17. That I really didn't want to. I had no strength left inside. I knew John would not put me out of my misery. Slowly, I lifted my legs, propping my feet up on the wall. I slipped my pant legs down, looking at the damage. Sliding my sleeves up, pulling my shirt up to see how bad it was. For weeks, I had ignored the damage done, refusing to look, refusing to acknowledge what he was doing to me. No more could I refuse to accept the reality of my situation. I simply wasn't going to make it, but there seemed to be no way out. I couldn't go on, not one more day. My love for my family wasn't enough to get me through this. My strength was gone, drained away. I knew I was trapped, at his mercy, and he had shown no mercy at all. But something had to change and I had no power to change anything.

I made it to a sitting position, staring out the window. The sun was getting lower in the sky. Soon, it would be night. John would be back to torture me more. I considered getting a beer. No, the fridge was too far. I didn't think I could walk anyway. Sitting there, looking down at the river rocks below me, I had a thought. "If I go out this window headfirst and land on those rocks, it would probably kill me. Even if it doesn't kill me, I would be paralyzed or so messed up, John wouldn't be able to take care of me. My parents would get me back or put me in some facility." I thought about that for a while. I tried to think of all the possibilities. If I was going to do this, it had to work. First, I had to be sure he couldn't go after Mark. Assessing the damage on my body, I felt pretty sure that John would be in trouble when I was found. *I could leave a note*, I thought. *No, he would destroy it.* I was sorry that it would hurt my family just before Mark's wedding, but I just couldn't hang on any longer. Maybe the wedding would bring celebration into their lives to help them through the grief?

There was a voice in my head, urging me to go out that window. "Do it!" the voice said. "Just open the window and slide out! Come on, it will be easy. All your pain will be gone. No more suffering! Do it! Go for it!" The voice made it difficult to think. My splitting headache also made thinking hard. It would surely end my pain and put a damper on John's plans. I was sure I would fit through the opening. I looked up at the sun shining. I felt like it was calling me to it. "Come on out and fly home!" it seemed to say. Home! Heaven! Living in glory, peace, and love with Jesus! Oh, how wonderful that sounded! I wanted to bask in that thought, but the voice was intruding. "Come on, you screwed this whole thing up! This is your chance to take control and do something right for a change. Hurry up or you'll miss your opportunity!" it urged.

My heart was pounding, my palms sweating. *Okay, Jesus, I'm coming home now*, I thought. I slid the little window open, gritting my teeth as my whole body screamed in protest. I pushed on the little screen. It bulged a bit. I shoved with my feet, and it popped out, falling to the rocks below. Slowly, I turned and stretched out, forcing myself to move. "The pain will be over soon," the voice encouraged me. "You can do this! It has to be this way." Lying there, feeling the warm air washing over my face, was so soothing. I felt at peace. I looked down at the rocks. All my life, I've been afraid of heights, terrified really. But now there was no fear. There was just sunshine, a warm breeze, and the voice, always the voice, blocking out any other thoughts. It promised that this would be the solution to my problems. "Just slide out and let go!" it whispered. "You know you want to. You'll be safe, at peace—no more of this struggle."

My head slipped through the window, just making it. I glanced at the parking lot. The space where John's car should be was still empty. A thrill went through me for a split second. I could actually *do* this and *win!* I grabbed the edge of the window and pushed with my feet. Lying on my right side really hurt, but I wanted to keep the parking lot in sight. I pushed up a little and slid my right arm out. Bracing myself against the building with my right hand, I pulled myself out a little more. I eased my left shoulder and arm out. I pressed my arms against the building and window to draw more of my torso outside, pushing with my feet. I was sure my hips would fit since my shoulders had. A few more seconds and it would be over! I would have eternal peace and love. Take that, John! You stupid, worthless piece of garbage! You won't have me to kick around anymore!

And then I felt his hands on my ankles. They grabbed and roughly pulled on me. My right side scraped against the metal window frame, tearing the skin off. There was blinding pain in my ribs. I tried to kick, twisting my legs as much as I could, but he was too strong. I heard John's voice, although I couldn't make out what he was saying. There was a roaring in my ears. The voice in my head screamed, "Nooooo!" I couldn't hold on. He was winning, pulling me back in through the window, back into the pits of *hell!*

What happened next was blacked out for twenty-nine years. I knew it was at this point that I died inside completely. But I had absolutely no memory of it at all. I had been seeing a therapist to help me through a rough patch of flashbacks and nightmares. One night when I couldn't sleep, the entire episode played in my head like a movie I could not turn off. It had been locked in a room in my mind, boarded up and marked "Condemned." But God took the boards off and threw open the door. It was incredibly painful to watch, to relive what I did, what I said, but I also know the memory is true. And it needs to be told. I'm sorry, Jesus. Please forgive my temper tantrum.

When John pulled me back into that apartment, I was furious, livid. John was yelling at me. I was in such a rage. I don't remember feeling any pain. He dragged me across the floor to the foot of the bed. As I rolled over to scream at him, I saw in the corner of the room between the bedroom and closet doors, a light. It filled the corner of the room from floor to beyond the ceiling. It was gloriously brilliant. Emanating from the light was love and peace like I had never experienced before. At that moment, I felt absolutely no pain. I knew it was the presence of God! He spoke to me in a calm, quiet voice, "Trust me." I have no idea how John could not see or hear him, but he did not. My rage increased and changed direction. I couldn't believe he had stopped me from coming home! He had allowed John to pull me back in to this living hell! What good could possibly come from my continued torture? I screamed with all my might at Jesus, my Savior. "I hate you, I hate you, *I hate you!* Damn you to hell! How dare you do this to me! I won't do it! I won't live through this!" Still, he stayed there in the corner, saying, "Trust me, let me help you. I'm here. Take my strength. Trust me." But I wouldn't. I was livid that *my* plan had been thwarted. John wouldn't kill me. God wouldn't let me die. No! It couldn't be! I *would* die! And I did. I knew Jesus would stay with me. He would never leave me nor forsake me. So I left him. I totally rejected him, his help, his love. I retreated so far into myself, I was like a zombie.

I no longer felt anything: pain, hunger, nothing could touch me. John had been screaming and punching me this whole time. I'm sure he thought my words had been directed at him. As I pulled into myself and became quiet, it seemed like I was outside my body. I could watch what happened to me and not even be affected. The light was gone. John calmed down. He seemed spent. I lay on the floor staring straight ahead, slowly blinking now and then. I was on my left side. The right side of my shirt was bloody. John told me to clean myself up and get ready for lessons. He left the room. I slowly followed and sat in my spot on the couch. He opened two beers and came in the living room. "I said 'clean up'!" he yelled. I stared straight ahead, blinking slowly. "Don't pull this shit on me anymore! I'm sick of it!" He grabbed my arm and pulled me into the bathroom. "Change your shirt and clean up *now!*" he ordered. I peed, took off the bloody shirt, and dug a dirty one from the hamper. Back in the living room, I started on my beer. I was sitting in my spot again, staring straight ahead.

He tried so hard that night to get a response from me, but he never did. He finally left me alone. I drank myself to sleep. I missed work the next day. Again, he did his worst, trying to make me talk, cry, beg, something, anything. The only success he had was making me vomit after he let me eat. Monday, I went to work. I didn't talk to anyone. I did eat a piece of pizza. John left me alone. I drank myself to sleep. I didn't eat again in that apartment. Tuesday, I went to work. I was like an automaton, a robot.

I felt no pain. I spoke when asked questions. I did my work and left with John. Tuesday night was the last time I slept in that apartment.

Wednesday and Thursday were the same. John glared at me a lot. He yelled and hit me. He put matches out on me. He didn't try raping me anymore. He screamed that my staring creeped him out. "Stop staring like that!" he demanded. "Say something!" I just took another swig of beer, still staring straight ahead, blinking now and then. He tried to interest me in TV. He brought Tippy over for me to pet. I ignored him. John lost it and threw Tippy outside. For all I knew, he had thrown him over the railing. No response. He took Ken out and threatened to open the door and let him fly away. No response. He stomped over to the door, put Ken on the floor, and opened the door. Tippy ran in and Ken flew back to his cage. It would have been funny if I had been alive, but I just stared straight ahead, drinking my beer.

He kept me up all night Wednesday and Thursday. No food, not even to play the "How many…" games. "You don't get to sleep until you cooperate, bitch!" he said. "I will make you talk. I'm in control! Not you. I will break you!" But I was already broken, empty, dead. He was just too stupid to see it. He slept while I worked. I didn't need to sleep. I was dead. Friday, he said he was going out with the neighbor and I was going to babysit again. All day, I stayed in my spot, smoking and drinking coffee. The neighbor lady came over with her daughter. I don't remember anything that was said by me or the girl. She went to bed at 8:00 p.m. and I started drinking.

John and the neighbor came back about 1:30 a.m. He had brought more beer. He said we were going to party at our place. The he slapped his forehead. "Cigarettes!" he exclaimed. "I forgot to buy some. I'll be right back." As he headed to the door, I said, "Don't lock us in." He gave me a warning look and said, "Of course not!" The neighbor said, "You better not lock me in!" He left. A few minutes later, I heard a scrape and the deadbolt slide, then feet pounding down the walkway. The neighbor jumped up and ran to the door, pounding on it. She yelled at John to come back. She was really mad. I just stared straight ahead.

"How can you just sit there?" she asked. "He locked us in!"

"He always locks me in," I replied.

"I'm calling my husband. He'll get Barb to let us out," she said.

"He took the phone," I answered. "He takes it every time he leaves." She was shocked.

"How can you put up with that?" she asked.

"That's the least of it," I said. For the next two hours, we drank and I filled her in on what John had been doing to me. She filled me in on what John had been saying about me. He had told her and Barb that my brother, Mark, had raped me and I had nightmares, but I was "seeing someone" about it. He told others it was my dad who had raped me and still others that it was both Dad and Mark. So that apparently explained away my screaming. Everyone thought he was such a saint for putting up with me and all my problems. I don't remember everything I told her, but I do remember that I didn't shed a single tear. I just sat there calmly, without any emotion, like we were discussing the weather. I have no idea why I chose to disclose all this to her. I really wasn't looking to be rescued. I was beyond that hope at this point. The only explanation I can come up with is it must have been the Lord speaking through me. She assured me that she was going to get me out. She and Barb would put a stop to this. But I was already out. I didn't answer her or argue with her.

She wondered out loud where John was, what he was doing all this time. I offered no comments. It didn't concern me. She checked on her daughter several times. She was still sleeping peacefully. Then John burst through the door, "Jennifer, get up and help me carry this gas BBQ up the stairs!" he demanded. The neighbor jumped up and started laying into him. They argued for a bit. She screamed about pressing charges. John screamed back. She headed down the hall to get her little girl, who amazingly was still asleep. John threw a beer bottle at her. It broke the hall light, sending glass all over. She kept going and came out with her daughter in her arms. John tried to stop her from leaving. They were both yelling. The little girl woke up crying. John tried to pull the girl from her mom's arms, desperate to keep her there, so he could "explain." She didn't want his explanations, she had heard enough! They played tug-of-war with the daughter. She cried and screamed, holding on to her mom. I sat in my spot, drinking, staring straight ahead. 19

Finally, the neighbor won the tug-of-war and ran out. John was right behind her. He grabbed a bike he had stolen and given to them. He screamed that they didn't deserve it and couldn't have it anymore. He brought it into our apartment. "Are you going to help me with this BBQ or not?" he yelled at me. I just took another swig of beer, staring straight ahead. He shook his head at me in disgust and left. I never moved from my spot the whole time all that drama played out in front of me. A little later, John came back with the phone. He called the police and said his apartment manager had tried to punch him. He wanted to press charges, but he wanted the cops to meet him at his parent's house. He said for them to not show up for thirty minutes. He repeated this twice to the operator. Then he hung up and ran out.

Barb came to the door a little later. I got up and sat by the door, opening the little window to talk to her. "What are you hiding in there? Why won't you let me in?" she demanded. "I'm not hiding anything," I replied. "I can't let you in. John locked me in and I have no key."

"Well, I'm sick of all the complaints and hassle," she said. "This is your ten-day notice. I'm evicting you guys." She left. I changed into my dorm shirt and sat back in my spot. The phone rang, dragging me out of the fog I was in. It was Barb. She asked if I wanted out. What a question! Did I? I didn't care. It couldn't possibly matter if I stayed or left, but Barb seemed to think I should leave. She said she would be up with her key. I put a change of clothes in a paper bag and waited.

When Barb unlocked the door, she said the neighbor was in her apartment and very upset. She took me down to her place. I sat on her couch next to her girlfriend. Barb and the neighbor were talking about the night and John's bizarre behavior. This was a new side of him that neither one had seen before. I listened quietly. Barb was flabbergasted and in disbelief at what the neighbor told her. She said it didn't even sound like the same person. She said she had heard a car crash and ran out to look. John had jumped out of his car and took a swing at her. She ducked back into her apartment and slammed the door. Apparently, that's when he came up and called the cops on her. Oh! Maybe Barb should know that. I told her and she responded, "But he attacked me!"

"It doesn't matter," I said. "The cops will believe him. They always do." So Barb called the cops on John. 13

I didn't want to go over everything with Barb, so I let the neighbor repeat what I had told her. They both kept saying it just couldn't be true. It had to be a fluke, a one-time event. The John they knew would never do these things. I explained that they had only met "Public" John. He is very different from "Private" John. Barb noticed I was still in my dorm shirt and suggested I go change before the cops got there. I went into their bedroom and changed. 13

The cops showed up with John. He had brought the ones he talked to at his parent's house. They arrived at the same time as the ones Barb called. They all had a mini conference outside first to try and sort things out. Then two cops entered Barb's apartment to take statements. John went up to our place with some other cops. That's when he lost it. He found out I wasn't there. He came tearing down the stairs, screaming my name, demanding to know where I was. I heard a cop outside tell him to calm down. He said he would find me for John. I told the cops in Barb's apartment not to let John know I was there.

It was the first time I had spoken since the cops showed up. They had been listening to the neighbor and Barb describing John's out-of-control actions of the previous night. Both said they wanted to press charges.

Now the cops looked at me. "What's she got to do with any of this?" the older one asked. The neighbor said I should be pressing charges too. The cop asked me what John had done to me. I looked at both of them—one was in his mid-forties, the other looked like a rookie. I had no idea what to say, how to explain the past six weeks. I turned my back and pulled my shirt up. I heard gasps and retching sounds. I straightened my shirt and turned back around. The rookie looked green. The older one was saying to Barb, "I've been a cop for twenty-three years, and I have never in my life seen anything like that!" He turned to me and said, "Don't you worry, we won't let him in here. You're safe now." They went outside and talked to the other cops.

John was handcuffed and put in a patrol car. A different cop came in and showed me John's prescription bottle. It was a big bottle that held about three hundred pills. He had just gotten it filled a few days ago and it was nearly half gone! He asked if I knew anything about it. I said he had written the prescription himself. I said I was sure he was addicted to codeine. John had tossed the bottle in the rocks under the stairs to try and hide it. But it was light out now and the cops had picked it up. I was taken to a cop car. We followed the other cops to John's parent's house. I told the cops I was riding with about the stolen BBQ unit John had hid in his dad's shed. But his dad wouldn't give permission for them to look, so they didn't find it. The neighbor had also mentioned it. I don't know if he ever was charged with that theft or not. Then we all drove to the police station. I was there for hours. They wanted all kinds of details on John's thefts. My only concern was the grace period not being up yet. Could John really refile assault charges against Mark? The cops assured me he would be in so much trouble for the next few months, he wouldn't be able to do anything to my brother.

Finally, they dropped me off back at the apartment. Barb let me in. I called Shelley and said, "Find someone with a truck. I'm moving out!" I hung up and started tossing stuff in boxes and paper bags. God bless Shelley! She got her dad and a friend over there in less than an hour. They moved me out, back to my parent's house. John's mom called before Shelley got there. She asked for John and I replied that he was in jail. She wanted to know why I wasn't in jail. I said I had done nothing wrong. "Oh, so that's how it is!" she snapped and hung up. I shrugged and went back to packing.

I only took what was left of my stuff. I did find a few of my butter and steak knives hidden here and there. Shelley's dad asked about the HBO unit and TV. I told him they were both stolen and I didn't want them. He asked if he could have them. I told him to go ahead and take them. They didn't belong to John, so as far as I was concerned, they were up for grabs. I didn't have any money to give him for gas, so that seemed like a fair trade to me. I had forgotten about the money I hid until weeks later.

My parents were out of town that weekend. It must have been Memorial Day weekend. I had put my stuff into my sister's old room that was now the guest room. I didn't want John to see my stuff in my room and know where I was. My room was on the front of the house and still had a broken window. The guest room was on the back of the house. I was out back by the pool, smoking, when Mark got home. He and his fiancée were house-sitting. He didn't seem happy to see me. He asked if I was allowed to move back. He didn't want to get in trouble with Mom and Dad. I said Mom had assured me I could always come home. He seemed satisfied with that answer and went back inside.

They were eating dinner when I came back in. I went to the guest room. We were pretty uncomfortable around each other. I was feeling at a loss. It had all happened so fast. One minute, I was in the apartment, dead and waiting to be finished off. The next, I was back home, dead and wondering what came now. I had nowhere else to go. No one mentioned shelters or safe houses for battered women. The cops had promised they would call me when John was released. They said he might even have to stay in jail until the court date. Either way, they said he would be in big trouble if he did anything to me. None of that turned out to be true. In the meantime, I was running on empty. I had no plans, no ideas, no thoughts of the future. I decided to get a beer.

In the kitchen, Mark asked me if I was hungry. I said, "No." Donna, his fiancée, nudged him. He asked when I had last eaten. Obviously, I did not look healthy to them. I stopped and stared for a minute. "What day is it?" I asked. "Saturday, it's Saturday night," he answered. I thought really hard. "Monday," I replied, "I ate on Monday."

Donna gasped and looked shocked, although I couldn't think why she would be. Mark asked if I would eat some chicken if he fixed it for me. "I'll try," I replied. He heated some up in the microwave and put it in front of me. I did not feel hungry at all, but I figured I better eat or they would be worried. I managed to eat a few bites. My stomach protested. I was very shaky and felt like I was going to be sick. "I can't eat anymore. Thanks anyway," I said. As I walked away, I heard Donna talking to Mark. The only word I made out was "anorexic." *I'm not anorexic!* I thought. I didn't have to be. John was anorexic for me!

Mark called me back. "How much do you weigh?" he asked.

"Now, or normally?" I tried to clarify.

"Both!" he said. He sounded mad. I didn't want him to be mad.

"I weigh 95 pounds. That's what I've weighed for the last two years," I answered. Donna had me get on the scale. It said 69 pounds. "That can't be right!" she exclaimed. She and Mark each weighed themselves. The scale read their correct weights. They put me back on it. The scale read 69 pounds again. They seemed really upset by that. I just got my beer and went out back for a smoke. It was no big deal to me. Corpses don't weigh much, I reasoned.

I didn't sleep more than an hour total Saturday night. What little sleep I got was in bits and pieces, just a few minutes at a time. The nightmares were intense and the flashbacks were relentless. It was like I was still trapped in that hell, even though I wasn't in the apartment. I stayed up late. I couldn't relax. I might have looked calm on the outside, but on the inside, I was a nervous wreck. It really freaked me out to have Mark at my parent's house. What if John was let out and he did something to Mark. I was sure he would come over here and start trouble. The last thing I wanted was to cause Mark more problems, but I didn't know what to do. I had run home on instinct and my brain couldn't come up with any solutions to the situation, so I just drank. I was just waiting for John to show up and end it all.

I tried to organize my stuff in the spare room. I put some boxes in my closet, figuring they wouldn't be seen from the outside in there. I found the PDR John stole in with my books. It had been packed by mistake. Sunday morning, I called the cops to turn it in. I didn't feel right about keeping it. I'm sure the cops who showed up thought I was crazy or on drugs or maybe both. I rambled on about John stealing the PDR, HBOs, BBQs; torturing me; pressing charges against Mark. I asked if he was still in jail. They didn't know anything about it. They took me back to the apartment to look at the stolen electronics in his dresser. He had told the first cops that I had stolen all of it! For all I knew my fingerprints were all over the stuff. He could have had me touching everything during a blackout. The cops didn't take any of the stolen goods. They didn't seem to care much about any of my story. Maybe they thought I was making things up to get attention. They did ask about the bathroom door. I just said I lost my temper. Going back to the apartment with them was a waste of time. But at least, I had turned in the PDR and told them where John took it from. I had done my duty.

Sunday, I tried to eat some. I was a wreck. John called my parent's house that afternoon. He had been bailed out by his mommy. He told me if I continued with pressing charges, he would rape my baby sister. I was sure he would do that. She was only fourteen! She had never even had a boyfriend yet. Having been raped repeatedly by him, I was *not* going to let him do that to her. I was so upset, I couldn't hold down the little I had forced myself to eat. Around 4:00 p.m., I realized it was Sunday. I was supposed to be at work that minute! No way could I make it. Even if I had a ride and time to get there, I was shaking and trembling constantly. I jumped at every noise. Whenever the phone rang, I dropped whatever I was holding at the time. I called in sick and told my supervisor I would explain everything tomorrow. She wasn't very happy. I had already missed too much work the past few weeks. 20

Mark and Donna tried to get me to rest before Mom and Dad came home. I laid down in the living room. I did doze off for a bit. I woke up to hushed voices in the dining room. My parents were back with my two younger sisters. Mark and Donna had been filling them in on what they knew of the situation. "Mom!" I called out. She came in and sat on the edge of the couch. I sat up and we hugged. She started crying and it made me tear up some. "He hurt me!" I said. She was really crying hard now and said, "I know. I'm sorry. He's not going to hurt you anymore." I was completely drained. Mom sent me to bed. As I walked away, I heard her say I looked like a skeleton with skin stretched on it. I slept for over eighteen hours.

In a nationwide survey, 9.4 percent of high school students report being hit, slapped, or physically hurt on purpose by their boyfriend or girlfriend in the twelve months prior to the survey.[4]

One in ten high school students has experienced physical violence from a dating partner in the past year.[5]

About 35 percent of women who were raped as minors also were raped as adults compared to 14 percent of women without an early rape history.[6]

More than half of all college students (57 percent) say it is difficult to identify dating abuse.[7]

Nearly one in ten teens in relationships report to having a partner tamper with their social networking account (the most frequent form of harassment or abuse).[8]

Victims of digital abuse and harassment are 2 times as likely to be physically abused, 2.5 times as likely to be psychologically abused, and 5 times as likely to be sexually coerced.[9]

Only 4 percent experience digital abuse and harassment alone. So social media, texts, and e-mails don't seem to invite new abuse, they just provide abusive partners with a new tool. [10]

Approximately one-half of the protection orders obtained by women against intimate partners who physically assaulted them were violated. More than two-thirds of the restraining orders against intimate partners who raped or stalked the victim were violated.[11]

Epilogue

John left me mostly alone in the weeks before our court date. He did call to complain about the TV and HBO being missing. I said I had no key and therefore no way to lock the apartment. So it was too bad if some of his stolen junk got stolen from him. It wasn't his to begin with. "Just think of it as justice!" I told him and hung up.

I was having troubles of my own. Eating and keeping food down was proving to be difficult. It seems John had effectively trained my body to be bulimic. I had lost twenty-six pounds in six weeks, living on coffee, cigarettes, and beer. I don't recommend it. I didn't get back to ninety-five pounds for six years, not until after I had my first child. I wanted to eat, to be normal. I could only eat small amounts and had to struggle to keep from vomiting. The smallest amount of stress would cause me to feel nauseous. John made sure I had stress. He would sit at the bus stop in his car. When I saw him, he would point his finger at me like it was a gun and pretend to shoot me. The cops said that he wasn't doing anything illegal. They suggested I switch stops, but the only way I accomplished anything was through muscle memory. If I changed my bus route, I would get lost and not make it to work. I had lost the ability to think things through or figure out anything new. Every time he called me, I would vomit.

Since the cops weren't stopping John from harassing me, I didn't think they would take serious his threat to rape my little sister. When our court date came, I was not there. Barb and the neighbor were mad at me for not showing up. John then became bolder in his harassment. He would call and ask me out. When I refused, he would immediately fly into a rage. "Why not?" he demanded. "What did I ever do to you, bitch?" He was still calling dozens of times a day and staking out my bus stops. The cops told me to stop calling them about it. They said he could do anything he wanted to me since I wasn't going to press charges. Mom got mad in September and talked to the detective in charge. She asked what it would take for them to arrest John. He was showing up at my window in the middle of the night, calling dozens of times a day, threatening me and my family. He killed Tippy and lit him on fire, then threw him into the bushes in front of my window. Mom had made me move back into my room since John knew I was there anyway. The cops told Mom that it was a civil dispute between a boyfriend and girlfriend and that nothing he was doing was illegal. "So we just wait until he kills her?" Mom asked. 27

"Well, then we would arrest him because killing her would be illegal," he answered. He said the police couldn't waste time and manpower on things like this because the girl never followed through with charges. He said we would just get back together before the court date, and I would drop everything again. Or he said John might finally leave us alone if he met someone else. It would just take time. "This has been going on for four months now!" Mom exclaimed.

"Well, that is quite a while, but there's nothing we can do, unless he actually breaks the law." Apparently, trespassing on our property, killing pets, making death threats, and harassing phone calls wasn't breaking the law!

I saw Paul once more. He came over to my parent's house sometime that summer. I can't remember when exactly. I was still pretty much dead. I lived for alcohol and nothing else. He asked how I was and if I was planning on going back to John again. I don't remember what I said to him other than "I'm sorry." Later, he and Shelley dated for a while. That bothered me, but really I had no claim to him. The last I heard of him, his ex-fiancée from back east came out to Phoenix and they got back together. I hope he had a great life. He was such a nice guy.

In October, I moved in with Mark and Donna. They were helped out financially with my rent money. This also gave Mom and Dad some peace. John stopped bothering them as much, once he figured out I was no longer there. It was hard to adjust to a new bus route, but I finally did. I even got a different job, working during the day. Mark and I were starting to repair our relationship.

Thirteen months after I was rescued, John shot himself and told the cops that Mark had done it. At this time, I was hiding in another state over a thousand miles away.

John had broken into my parent's house and found a letter I had written them. He realized I was physically out of his reach, so he did what was in his twisted mind the next best thing to torture me. He went after my brother, again, for something he did not do. Mark was arrested at work and charged with attempted murder. John survived five hours of surgery. The doctors told the cops after the surgery that his wound was self-inflicted. He had chatted up enough doctors to know where to shoot himself and live through it. Mark was released and the charges dropped, but the damage had been done. His marriage fell apart. He moved to another state and remarried. Then he lost his job and couldn't find another one. He was drinking a lot and depressed. He died of a self-inflicted gunshot at the age of thirty-one.

The last time I heard from John was two and a half years after I got away from him. He called my parent's house on Thanksgiving. He was bawling, saying he was really down and needed a friend. I said I had friends and the last thing I needed was him. I hung up, frantic. Where was he? Would he follow me back to my place? I lived alone, just me and my four cats. If I hadn't been so panicked, I might have realized that he was probably calling from jail. He never could stand being locked up and always cried like a baby, begging to get out. Instead, I let my ex-boyfriend, another abuser, move back in with me for protection. I made him sleep on the floor between the door and my bed. I figured if John broke in, he would trip over the lug on the floor and I could stab him with the knife I kept by my bed. I didn't find out until the next February that John had been calling from jail. 27

He had stolen checks from his mom and was forging them for his spending money. When her checks started bouncing, she was forced to press charges against him or take the rap for the bum checks herself. So she finally had to stand up to her precious little baby and make him take responsibility for his actions. Meanwhile, I had this jerk ex-boyfriend back in my place, leeching off me. It took a while, but I finally kicked him out.

I was addicted to alcohol until I was twenty-nine. It took years before I was alive enough to have an opinion about things, like what I liked on my pizza, clothes, music, what to hang on the walls. I had no idea who I was. I got tired of saying, "I don't know," when asked these kinds of questions, so I started saying, "I don't care." Much of what happened in that apartment was blacked out before I started writing this. I really wasn't sure how to write about the blackouts, but Jesus brought to my memory many things and wrote it for me. The rape in the shower, the rape with the stimulator, and the belt incidents were completely blocked until the writing of this story. I wrote the words, stopped, read what I had written and knew the truth of it. Ever since John, the sound of a belt buckle clinking has brought me a sense of panic and fear. I never knew why until Jesus brought this memory back for me. There is still a lot blacked out, but I have no desire to remember more. Some things are better left in the dark. If Jesus needs me to know it, he will bring it back for me.

Over the years, I was suicidal off and on. Satan still whispering in my ear to end it all, that I was no good, trying to destroy me. When I finally gave Jesus control of my life, he began to heal me. He took a terrified wretch with no hope and made her into a strong, confident, joyful lady. My prayer is that he will bring good from the bad as only he can do. I give him all the glory for the changes he has made in me. He is my strength, my shield, my deliverer, my rock, my hiding place, my loving, forgiving Savior! In him fully do I trust, finally!

There are two things in my story that bring me the most shame. The first is not helping the neighbor with her daughter during the tug-of-war with John. To just sit there while that child was being pulled back and forth is unthinkable. I love children! I always have. She was helpless and so terrified, and I just sat there sipping beer. All I can say is I was so dead inside that I didn't feel anything at the time. I pray she and her mom can forgive me.

The second thing brings me the most shame of anything in my life. That is my rejection of my Savior, Jesus Christ. I had *no* right to lose my temper with him. It is unfathomable that I cursed him, telling him to go to hell. He would have been justified in wiping me off the planet! But he forgave me! It is unimaginable that an awesome, *holy* God, worthy of all worship, honor, and praise, would take the abuse I dished out that day when John pulled me back in through the window. Not only did Jesus take that from me, he stayed with me through all my foolishness. He never left my side, though I refused to see or acknowledge him. He graciously and lovingly welcomed me back to him when I finally came to the end of my idiotic running from him. If he would have let me have my way that day, this story would probably not be told. All the good he is going to bring from it would not come about.

He saved me from my sin and I wallowed in it. I dragged my Savior through hell because I would not leave it and he would not leave me! On top of all that, he picks me up, cleans me off, and loves me with an everlasting love! I'm sure I could have been rescued earlier, if I would only have cried out to him and accepted his help. Over the years, he has rescued me from my stupidity and stubborn sinfulness many times. I can't go back and change the past. I don't know that I would if given the chance. But I can let Jesus take that past and use it to help others. If you read this and walk away, thinking, "Wow, poor her," and don't believe it could happen to you, then I have failed. My purpose in all this is to show the abusive pattern of behavior so you can spot an abuser early and not get involved with one. That is the purpose of the index at the back. The page numbers give an example of that specific behavior. The paragraph on the page is marked with the corresponding behavior on the index.

Please learn from my story, my mistakes. Learn the warning signs of an abuser. They have a recognizable pattern of behavior! Over the years, I've talked to many ladies who have suffered like me and we came to this conclusion—all these guys are the same! Their behavior is so similar, they could be the same guy! You just change the name and physical description, but the pattern is there. Learn how they act, the things they say, the methods of control they use and steer clear of these demons. Don't get involved with them! Leave them no one to abuse! You don't deserve to be hit or controlled or abused. You can't change them or love them into changing. The more you try to please them, the more they will demand of you. Every time you cave in to their demands, they will respect you less. They don't even respect themselves. If you allow them to control you, they will control you to death! They know they don't deserve any respect and will see you as less than themselves because you give in to them. Your own sweet behavior will trap you before you realize you have been trapped. Once he hits you, it is too late to safely leave. You can escape, but it is much more dangerous and complicated.

Jesus wants you to live a victorious life—full of joy, peace, and love. He created you, loves you dearly, and has a plan for you. His plan is for your good, not to destroy you or hurt you. Don't let Satan get a victory by stealing God's perfect will for you! Satan only wants to steal, kill, and destroy. He is a liar who wants to trap you with his lies! There is no truth in him. He has no right to take anything from you unless you give him the right by listening to his lies. Seek Jesus and his truth. His truth will make you free!

For more information or to get help, please call:

The National Domestic Violence Hotline at 1-800-799-7233

The National Sexual Assault Hotline at 1-800-656-4673

The National Teen Dating Abuse Hotline at 1-866-331-9474

Acknowledgments

There are so many people who have helped me in writing my story, I hope that I don't skip a name. I give credit first to my precious Savior, Jesus Christ. He knows how deep and black the pit was that he saved me from and he alone has equipped me to tell my story. Many people over the years have encouraged, supported and prayed for me. I appreciate everyone who read the rough drafts and gave me suggestions and shared their insights: most especially, Alison, Becky, Beth, Bob, Brit, Ciara, Joe, Jolene, Maura, Misti, Renea, Rhonda, Robin and Sheila. I also would like to thank the staff and advocates at the sexual assault organization, my supportive family and my loving church family. Many thanks to all the helpful, patient folks at Tate Publishing.

Index of Behaviors

Please use this index to become familiar with the behaviors abusers use. It may save your life or the life of a loved one! Go to the page number indicated for an example of that specific behavior. At the end of the paragraphs, you will find the number that corresponds to the behavior.

1. Minimizes your feelings 14, 17, 19, 20, 22-25, 27-28, 30-31, 33-36, 41-43, 51-53, 66-68, 127-128, 143.
2. Excessive and quick commitment to relationships 15, 17, 20.
3. Isolates you from family and friends 16, 17, 20-22, 24, 28-29, 31-32, 49, 98, 125-126, 138.
4. Dominates your time 15, 20-22, 27-30, 33-34, 41-42, 57, 73.
5. Scares you by driving recklessly 16, 31-33, 61-62.
6. Threatens to break up with you to control you 13-14, 23, 24, 25, 37-38, 42-43.

7. Extremely possessive and jealous 20-22, 24-25, 31-32, 36-37, 50, 61-62, 69-70, 77.

8. Name-calling and demeaning 17, 18, 19, 22-25, 27-28, 31-32, 35-37, 45, 61-62, 69-70, 102, 108, 112, 120, 175.

9. Excessive monitoring 15, 20-22, 33-34, 63-64, 72-73.

10. Insecure, but presents a false sense of superiority 11, 13-14, 17, 19, 20, 22, 24-26, 29, 33, 39, 47-49, 50, 61, 72-73.

11. Extremely controlling behavior early on, disguised as concern for safety 22-25, 33-34, 66.

12. Lack of empathy 14, 22-23, 27-28, 36-38, 52-53, 61-62, 67-68, 81.

13. Presents dual personalities 11, 16, 17, 18-19, 24, 26, 27-29, 47-48, 52-55, 63-64, 70, 78, 80, 92, 104, 176-177.

14. Extreme angry outbursts 17, 18, 22-23, 26-28, 31-33, 38, 47-48, 52, 68-69, 71-72, 77, 83.

15. Blames temper on others or alcohol/drugs 32-33, 38, 56-57, 101-102, 136.

16. Has unrealistic expectations or demands 13, 17, 18, 22-28, 31-38, 40-44, 47-49, 66, 70, 77.

17. Hypersensitivity and victim mentality 16, 17, 22-23, 24, 25, 27-29, 31-35, 38, 40, 42-44, 47, 52, 55-56.

18. Takes away choices such as food, fashion, social life 18, 20, 22, 24, 25, 28, 33-36, 38, 41-47, 51-53, 65, 66, 68, 78, 81, 92, 120, 142, 155.

19. Exhibits cruelty to children or animals 51-52, 56-58, 61, 68-69, 101, 114, 154, 175.

20. Threats against you, your children, or of suicide for failure to comply 32-33, 40-41, 44, 54, 57-58, 72-73, 77-78, 87-88, 100-101, 154, 183.

21. Blames the victim 25, 40-43, 51-52, 56-57, 62-63, 66, 68-69, 70, 90-91, 104, 111, 123-124, 134, 158-159, 165-166.

22. Control of all money 22, 25, 38-39, 45-46, 52-53, 68-69, 107, 147, 152.

23. Restrains you or keeps you from leaving a dangerous/uncomfortable situation 16, 50-53, 55-56, 61-62, 70-72, 92, 93-94, 98, 115.

24. Rewrites personal history at will 27-29, 30-31, 36, 39, 52, 58-59, 62-63, 68-70, 166.

25. Extreme sense of entitlement 13-14, 25, 26-27, 30, 32-33, 42, 52-53, 57-59, 70-72, 77-78, 81, 83, 89, 98-99, 112, 142.

26. Poor communication skills 16, 18, 19, 21, 23, 25-26, 31-33, 36-37, 45-48, 61, 70, 72-73.

27. Expects unlimited second chances 14, 15, 26-27, 32, 52, 63, 72-73, 77, 78, 165, 186, 188.

Notes

1. http://www.cdc.gov/violenceprevention/pdf/nisvs_report2010-a.pdf
2. http://www.bjs.gov/content/pub/pdf/ipv9310.pdf
3. http://annalsofepidemiology.org/article/S1047-2797(12)00024-5/abstract
4. http://www.cdc.gov/violenceprevention/intimatepartnerviolence/teen_dating_violence.html
5. http://www.cdc.gov/violenceprevention/pdf/datingmatters_flyer_2012-a.pdf
6. http://www.cdc.gov/violenceprevention/pdf/cdc_nisvs_overview_insert_final-a.pdf
7. http://www.loveisrespect.org/pdf/College_Dating_And_Abuse_Final_Study.pdf
8. http://www.urban.org/UploadedPDF/412750-teen-dating-abuse.pdf
9. http://www.urban.org/UploadedPDF/412750-teen-dating-abuse.pdf
10. http://www.urban.org/UploadedPDF/412750-teen-dating-abuse.pdf

11. Tjaden, Patricia & Thoennes, Nancy. National Institute of Justice and the Centers of Disease Control and Prevention, "Extent, Nature and Consequences of Intimate Partner Violence: Findings from the National Violence Against Women Survey" (2000).